Mayne Reid

The Castaways

A Story of Adventure in the Wilds of Borneo

Mayne Reid

The Castaways
A Story of Adventure in the Wilds of Borneo

ISBN/EAN: 9783744734219

Printed in Europe, USA, Canada, Australia, Japan

Cover: Foto ©Andreas Hilbeck / pixelio.de

More available books at **www.hansebooks.com**

THE CASTAWAYS:

A STORY

OF

ADVENTURE IN THE WILDS OF BORNEO,

BY

CAPTAIN MAYNE REID.

NEW YORK:
SHELDON & COMPANY,
498 & 500 BROADWAY,
1870.

Entered according to Act of Congress, in the year 1870,

BY SHELDON & CO.,

In the Office of the Librarian of Congress, at Washington.

CONTENTS.

		PAGE
I.	A Castaway Crew	7
II.	The Hammer-Head	13
III.	The Albatross	18
IV.	The Cry of the Dugong	24
V.	Running the Breakers	31
VI.	A Gigantic Oyster	36
VII.	A Dangerous Locality	43
VIII.	Shooting at Fruit	50
IX.	Gagging a Gavial	58
X.	Burrowing Birds	65
XI.	The Lanoons	77
XII.	Krissing a Constrictor	85
XIII.	Chicks quick to take Wing	90
XIV.	A Grand Tree-Climber	97
XV.	Something Sharp	106
XVI.	An Enemy in the Air	111
XVII.	Sitting by the Spit	118
XVIII.	Sick after Supper	126
XIX.	An Uneasy Night	131
XX.	The Deadly Upas	137
XXI.	Starting for the Interior	142
XXII.	Across Country	150
XXIII.	Tough Travelling	159
XXIV.	A Red Satyr	165
XXV.	Silence Restored	169

CONTENTS.

		PAGE
XXVI.	In Fear and Trembling	173
XXVII.	A Spectacle rarely Seen	180
XXVIII.	Still Trusting in God	186
XXIX.	A Captive carried Aloft	191
XXX.	What will become of Her?	197
XXXI.	The Pursuit Arrested	202
XXXII.	Listening in Despair	206
XXXIII.	Striking Out	212
XXXIV.	Swimming in Shadow	217
XXXV.	The Family at Home	221
XXXVI.	An Improvised Palanquin	226
XXXVII.	The Journey continued	230
XXXVIII.	The Friendly Flag	234

THE CASTAWAYS.

CHAPTER I.

A CASTAWAY CREW.

A BOAT upon the open sea—no land in sight!

It is an open boat, the size and form showing it to be the pinnace of a merchant-ship.

It is a tropical sea, with a fiery sun overhead, slowly coursing through a sky of brilliant azure.

The boat has neither sail nor mast. There are oars, but no one is using them. They lie athwart the tholes, their blades dipping in the water, with no hand upon the grasp.

And yet the boat is not empty. Seven human forms are seen within it—six of them living, and one dead.

Of the living, four are full-grown men; three of

them white, the fourth of an umber-brown, or *bistre* color. One of the white men is tall, dark, and bearded, with features bespeaking him either a European or an American, though their somewhat elongated shape and classic regularity would lead to a belief that he is the latter, and in all probability a native of New York. And so he is.

The features of the white man sitting nearest to him are in strange contrast to his, as is also the color of his hair and skin. The hair is of a carroty shade, while his complexion, originally reddish, through long exposure to a tropical sun, exhibits a yellowish, freckled appearance. The countenance so marked is unmistakably of Milesian type. So it should be, as its owner is an Irishman.

The third white man, of thin, lank frame, with face almost beardless, pale cadaverous cheeks, and eyes sunken in their sockets, and there rolling wildly, is one of those nondescripts who may be English, Irish, Scotch, or American. His dress betokens him to be a seaman, a common sailor.

He of the brown complexion, with flat spreading nose, high cheek-bones, oblique eyes, and straight, raven black hair, is evidently a native of the East, a Malay.

The two other living figures in the boat are those of a boy and girl. They are white. They differ but little in size, and but a year or two in age, the girl being fourteen and the boy about sixteen.

There is also a resemblance in their features. They are brother and sister.

The fourth white, who lies dead in the bottom of the boat, is also dressed in seaman's clothes, and has evidently in his lifetime been a common sailor.

It is but a short time since the breath departed from his body; and judging by the appearance of the others, it may not be long before they will all follow him into another world.

How weak and emaciated they appear, as if in the last stage of starvation! The boy and girl lie along the stern-sheets, with wasted arms, embracing each other. The tall man sits on one of the benches, gazing mechanically upon the corpse at his feet; while the other three also have their eyes upon it, though with very different expressions. That upon the face of the Irishman is of sadness, as if for the loss of an old shipmate; the Malay looks on with the impassive tranquillity peculiar to his race; while in the sunken orbs of the nondescript can be detected a look that speaks of a horrible craving—the craving of cannibalism.

The scene described, and the circumstances which have led to it, call for explanation. It is easily given. The tall dark-bearded man is Captain Robert Redwood, the skipper of an American merchant-vessel, for some time trading among the islands of the Indian Archipelago. The Irishman is his ship-carpenter, the Malay his pilot, while the others are two common sailors of his crew. The boy and girl are his children, who, having no mother or near relatives at home, have been brought along with him on his trading voyage to the Eastern Isles. The vessel passing from Manilla, in the Philippines, to the Dutch settlement of Macassar, in the island of Celebes, has been caught in a *typhoon* and swamped near the middle of the Celebes Sea; her crew have escaped in a boat—the pinnace—but saved from death by drowning, only to find, most of them, the same watery grave after long-procrastinated suffering from thirst, from hunger, from all the agonies of starvation.

One after another have they succumbed, and been thrown overboard, until the survivors are only six in number. And these are but skeletons, each looking as if another day, or even another hour, might terminate his wretched existence.

It may seem strange that the youthful pair in the stern-sheets, still but tender children, and the girl more especially, should have withstood the terrible suffering beyond a period possible to many strong men, tough sailors every one of them. But it is not so strange after all, or rather after knowing that, in the struggle with starvation, youth always proves itself superior to age, and tender childhood will live on where manhood gives way to the weakness of inanition.

That Captain Redwood is himself one of the

strongest of the survivors may be due partly to the fact of his having a higher organism than that of his ship-comrades. But, no doubt, he is also sustained by the presence of the two children, his affection for them and fear for their fate warding off despair, and so strengthening within him the principle of vitality.

If affection has aught to do with preserving life, it is strong enough in the Irishman to account also for the preservation of his; for although but the carpenter in Captain Redwood's ship, he regards the captain with a feeling almost fraternal. He had been one of his oldest and steadiest hands, and long service has led to a fast friendship between him and his old skipper.

On the part of the Irishman, this feeling is extended to the youthful couple who recline, with clasped hands, along the sternmost seat of the pinnace.

As for the Malay, thirst and hunger have also made their marks upon him; but not as with those of Occidental race. It may be that his bronze skin does not show so plainly the pallor of suffering; but, at all events, he still looks lithe and life-like, supple and sinewy, as if he could yet take a spell at the oar, and keep alive as long as skin and bone held together. If all are destined to die in that open boat, he will certainly be the last. He with the hollow eyes looks as if he would be the first.

Down upon this wretched group, a picture of misery itself, shines the hot sun of the tropics; around it, far as eye could reach, extends the calm sea, glassed, and glancing back his rays, as though they were reflected from a sheet of liquid fire; beneath them gleams a second firmament through the pellucid water, a sky peopled with strange forms that are not birds: more like are they to dragons; for among them can be seen the horrid form of the devil-fish, and the still more hideous figure of the hammer-headed shark. And alone is that boat above them, seemingly suspended in the air, and only separated from these dreadful monsters by a few feet of clear water, through which they can dart with the speed of electricity. Alone, with no land in sight, no ship or sail, no other boat—nothing that can give them a hope.

All bright above, around, and beneath; but within their hearts only darkness and the dread of death!

CHAPTER II.

THE HAMMER-HEAD.

FOR some time the castaways had been seated in moody silence, now and then glancing at the corpse in the bottom of the boat, some of them no doubt thinking how long it might be before they themselves would occupy the same situation.

But now and then, also, their looks were turned upon one another, not hopefully, but with a mechanical effort of despair.

In one of these occasional glances, Captain Redwood noticed the unnatural glare in the eyes of the surviving sailor, as also did the Irishman. Simultaneously were both struck with it, and a significant look was exchanged between them.

For a period of over twenty hours this man had been behaving oddly; and they had conceived something more than a suspicion of his insanity. The death of the sailor lying at the bottom of the boat, now the ninth, had rendered him for a time more tranquil, and he sat quiet on his seat, with elbows resting on his knees, his cheeks held between the palms of his hands. But the wild stare in his eyes seemed to have become only more intensified as he kept them fixed upon the corpse of his comrade. It was a look worse than wild; it had in it the expression of *craving*.

On perceiving it, and after a moment spent in reflection, the captain made a sign to the ship-carpenter, at the same time saying,—

"Murtagh, it's no use our keeping the body any longer in the boat. Let us give it such burial as the sea vouchsafes to a sailor,—and a true one he was."

He spoke these words quietly, and in a low tone, as if not intending them to be heard by the suspected maniac.

"A thrue sailor!" rejoined the Irishman. "Truth ye're roight there, captin. Och, now! to think he's the ninth of them we've throwed overboard, all the crew of the owld ship, exceptin' our three selves, widout countin' the Malay an' the childer. If it wasn't that yer honor's still left, I'd say the best goes first; for the nigger there looks as if he'd last out the whole lot of—"

The captain, to whom this imprudent speech was torture, with a gesture brought it to an abrupt termination. He was in fear of its effect not on the Malay, but on the insane sailor. The latter, however, showed no sign of having heard or understood it; and in a whisper Murtagh received instructions how to act.

"You lay hold of him by the shoulders," were the words spoken, "while I take the feet. Let us slip him quietly over without making any stir. Saloo, remain you where you are; we won't need your help."

This last speech was addressed to the Malay, and in his own language, which would not be understood by any other than himself. The reason for laying the injunction upon him was, that he sat in the boat beyond the man deemed mad, and his coming across to the others might excite the latter and bring about some vaguely dreaded crisis.

The silent Malay simply nodded an assent, showing no sign that he comprehended why his assistance was not desired. For all that, he understood it, he too having observed the mental condition of the sailor. Rising silently from their seats, and advancing toward the dead body, the captain and carpenter, as agreed upon, laid hold of and raised it up in their arms. Even weak as both were, it was not much of a lift to them. It was not a corpse, only a skeleton, with the skin still adhering, and drawn tightly over the bones.

Resting it upon the gunwale of the boat, they made a moment's pause, their eyes turned heavenward, as if mentally repeating a prayer.

The Irishman, a devout believer in the efficacy of outward observances, with one hand detached from the corpse, silently made the sign of the cross.

Then was the body again raised between them, held at arm's length outward, and tenderly lowered down upon the water.

There was no plunge, only a tiny plashing, as if a chair, or some other piece of light wood-work, had been dropped gently upon the surface of the sea. But slight as was the sound, it produced an effect, startling as instantaneous. The sailor, whose dead comrade was thus being consigned to the deep, as it were, surreptitiously, all at once sprang to his feet, sending forth a shriek that rang far over the tranquil water. With one bound, causing the pinnace to heel fearfully over, he placed himself by the side over which the corpse had been lowered, and stood with arms upraised, as if intending to plunge after it.

The sight underneath should have awed him. The dead body was slowly, gradually sinking, its garb of dark blue Guernsey shirt becoming lighter blue as it went deeper down in the cerulean water; while fast advancing to meet it, as if coming up from the darkest depths of the ocean, was a creature of monstrous shape, the very type of a monster. It was the hideous hammer-headed shark, the dreaded *zygæna* of the Celebes Sea.

With a pair of enormous eyes glaring sullenly out from two immense cheek-like protuberances, giving to its head that singular sledge-hammer appearance whence it has its name, it advanced directly toward the slow-descending corpse, itself, however, moving so rapidly that the spectators above had scarce taken in the outlines of its horrid form, when this was no longer visible. It was hidden in what appeared a shower of bluish pearls suddenly projected underneath the water, and enveloping both the dead body of the sailor and the living form of the shark. Through the dimness could be distinguished gleams of a pale phosphoric sheen like lightning flashes through a sky cloud; and soon after froth and bubbles rose effervescing upon the surface of the sea.

It was a terrible spectacle, though only of an instant's duration. When the subaqueous cloud cleared away, and they again looked with peering eyes down into the pellucid depths, there was nothing there, neither dead body of man, nor living form of monster. The *zygæna* had secured its prey, and carried the skeleton corpse to some dark cavern of the deep.*

* The hammer-headed shark, in common language, is rightly designated one of the most hideous of marine animals. We mean hideous in outward appearance, for, of course, there is much both wonderful and beautiful in its internal organization, and, in the exquisite fitness of its structure for its peculiar part in the economy of nature. In the general outline of its body, which is something like that of a cylinder, it resembles the ordinary sharks; and its distinctive feature is its head, which, on either side, expands like a double-headed hammer. The eyes are very large, and placed at each extremity. It is found in the Mediterranean Sea, as well as in the Indian Ocean, and is noted for its fierceness and voracity.

CHAPTER III.

THE ALBATROSS.

APTAIN REDWOOD and the Irishman were horrified at the sight that had passed under their eyes. So, too, were the children, who had both started up from their reclining attitude, and looked over the side of the boat. Even the impassive Malay, all his life used to stirring scenes, in which blood was often shed, could not look down into those depths, disturbed by such a tragical occurrence, without having aroused within him a sensation of horror.

All of them recoiled back into the boat, staggering down upon their seats. One alone remained standing, and with an expression upon his face as if he was desirous of again beholding the sight. It was not a look that betrayed pleasure, but one grim and ghastly, yet strong and steady, as if it penetrated the profoundest depths of the ocean. It was the look of the insane sailor.

If his companions had still held any lingering doubts about his insanity, it was sufficient to dispel them. It was the true stare of the maniac.

It was not long continued. Scarce had they resumed their seats when the man, once more elevating his arms in the air, uttered another startling shriek, if possible louder and wilder than before. He had stepped upon one of the boat seats, and stood with body bent, half leaning over the gunwale, in the attitude of a diver about to make his headlong plunge.

There could be no mistaking his intention to leap overboard, for his comrades could see that his muscles were strained to the effort.

All three—the captain, Murtagh, and the Malay—suddenly rose again, and leant forward to lay hold on him. They were too late. Before a finger could touch him he had made the fatal spring; and the next moment he was beneath the surface of the sea!

None of them felt strong enough to leap after and try to save him. In all probability, the effort would have been idle, and worse; for the mad fancy that seemed urging him to self-destruction might still influence his mind, and carry another victim into the same vortex with himself. Restrained by this thought, they stood up in the boat, and watched for his coming up again.

He did so at length, but a good distance off. A breeze had been gradually springing up, and during his dive the pinnace had made some way, by drifting before it. When his head was again seen above the curling water, he was nearly a hundred yards to windward of the boat. He was not so far off as to prevent them from reading the expression upon his face, now turned toward them. It had become changed, as if by magic. The wild look of insanity was gone, and in its place was one almost equally wild, though plainly was it an expression of fear, or indeed terror. The immersion into the cold, deep sea, had told upon his fevered brain, producing a quick reaction of reason; and his cries for help, now in piteous tones sent back to the boat, showed that he understood the peril in which he had placed himself.

They were not unheeded. Murtagh and the Malay rushed, or rather tottered to the oars; while the captain threw himself into the stern, and took hold of the tiller-ropes.

In an instant the pinnace was headed round, and moving through the water in the direction of the swimmer, who, on his side, swam toward them, though evidently with feeble stroke. There seemed not much doubt of their being able to pick him up. The only danger thought of by any of them was the *zygæna;* but they hoped the shark might be still occupied with its late prey, and not seeking another victim. There might be another shark, or many more; but for some time past one only had been seen in the neighborhood of the boat; the shark, as they supposed, which had but recently devoured the dead body of the sailor. Trusting to this conjecture, they plied the oars with all the little strength left in their arms. Still, notwithstanding their feeble efforts, and the impediment of pulling against the wind, they were nearing the unfortunate man, surely, if slowly.

They had got over half the distance; less than half a cable's length was now between the boat and the struggling swimmer. Not a shark was to be seen on the water, nor beneath it—no fish of any kind—nothing whatever in the sea. Only, in the sky above, a large bird, whose long scimitar-shaped wings and grand curving beak told them what it was—an albatross. It was the great albatross of the Indian seas, with an extent of wing beyond that of the largest eagle, and almost equalling the spread of the South American condor.*

They scarce looked at it, or even glanced above; they were looking below for the *zygæna*—scanning

* The albatross is the largest of the ocean-birds, its wings, when extended, measuring fifteen feet, and its weight sometimes exceeding twenty to twenty-four pounds. The common albatross is the *Diomedea exulans* of naturalists. Its plumage, except a few of the wing feathers, is white; its long, hard beak, which is very powerful, is of a pale yellow color; and its short, webbed feet are flesh-colored. It is frequently met with in the Southern Ocean. The species mentioned in the text is the black-beaked albatross, which frequents the Indian waters. The albatross is a formidable enemy to the sailor, for if one falls overboard, he will assuredly fall a victim to this powerful bird, unless rescued immediately by his comrades. Its cry has some resemblance to that of the pelican; but it will also, when excited, give vent to a noise not unlike the braying of an ass. The female makes a rude nest of earth on the sea-shore, and deposits therein her solitary egg, which is about four inches long, white, and spotted at the larger end.

the surface of the water around them, or with their eyes keenly bent, endeavoring to penetrate its indigo depths in search of the monstrous form.

No shark in sight. All seemed well; and despite the piteous appeals of the swimmer, now toiling with feebler stroke, and scarce having power to sustain himself, they in the pinnace felt sure of being able to rescue him.

Less than a quarter cable's length lay between. The boat, urged on by the oars, was still lessening the distance. Five minutes more, and they would be close to their comrade, and lift him over the gunwale.

Still no *zygœna* in sight—no shark of any kind.

"Poor fellow! he seems quite cured; we shall be able to save him."

It was Captain Redwood who thus spoke. The Irishman was about making a little hopeful rejoinder, when his speech was cut short by a cry from Saloo, who had suspended his stroke, as if paralyzed by some sudden despair.

The Malay, who, as well as Murtagh, had been sitting with his back toward the swimmer, had slewed himself round with a quick jerk, that told of some surprise. The movement was caused by a shadow flitting over the boat; something was passing rapidly through the air above. It had caught the attention of the others, who, on hearing Saloo's cry, looked up along with him.

They saw only the albatross moving athwart the sky, no longer slow sailing as before, but with the swift-cutting flight of a falcon pouncing down upon its prey. It seemed descending not in a straight line, but in an acute parabolic curve, like a thunderbolt or some aërolite projected toward the surface of the sea. But the bird, with a whirr like the sound of running spindles, was going in a definite direction, the point evidently aimed at being the head of the swimmer!

A strange commingled shout arose over the ocean, in which several voices bore part. Surprise pealed forth from the lips of those in the boat, and terror from the throat of the struggling man, while a hoarse croak from the gullet of the albatross, followed by what appeared a mocking scream of triumph. Then quick succeeded a crashing sound, as the sharp, heavy beak of the bird broke through the skull of the swimmer, striking him dead, as if by the shot of a six-pounder, and sending his lifeless body down toward the bottom of the sea!

It came not up again—at all events, it was never more seen by his castaway companions; who, dropping the oars in sorrowful despair, allowed the boat to drift away from the fatal spot—in whatever direction the soft-sighing breeze might capriciously carry it.

CHAPTER IV.

THE CRY OF THE DUGONG.

NTIL the day on which the ninth sailor had died of starvation, and the tenth had been struck dead by the sea-bird, the castaways had taken an occasional spell at the oars. They now no longer touched, nor thought of them. Weakness prevented them, as well as despondency. For there was no object in continuing the toil; no land in sight, and no knowledge of any being near. Should a ship chance to come their way, they were as likely to be in her track lying at rest, as if engaged in laboriously rowing. They permitted the oars, therefore, to remain motionless between the thole pins, themselves sitting listlessly on the seats, most of them with their heads bent despairingly downward. The Malay alone kept his shining black eyes on the alert, as despair had not yet prostrated him.

The long sultry day that saw the last of their two sailor comrades, at length came to a close, without any change in their melancholy situation.

The fierce hot sun went down into the bosom of the sea, and was followed by the short tropic twilight. As the shades of night closed over them, the father, kneeling beside his children, sent up a prayer to Him who still held their lives in His hand; while Murtagh said the Amen; and the dark-skinned Malay, who was a Mohammedan, muttered a similar petition to Allah. It had been their custom every night and morning, since parting from the foundered ship, and during all their long-protracted perils in the pinnace.

Perhaps that evening's vesper was more fervent than those preceding it; for they felt they could not last much longer, and that all of them were slowly, surely dying.

This night, a thing something unusual, the sky became obscured by clouds. It might be a good omen, or a bad one. If a storm, their frail boat would run a terrible risk of being swamped; but if rain should accompany it, there might be a chance of collecting a little water upon a tarpaulin that lay at the bottom.

As it turned out, no rain fell, though there arose what might be called a storm. The breeze, springing up at an early hour of the day, commenced increasing after sunset.

It was the first of any consequence they had encountered since taking to the boat; and it blew right in the direction whither they intended steering.

With the freshening of the wind, as it came cool upon his brow, the castaway captain seemed to become inspired with a slight hope. It was the same with Murtagh and the Malay.

"If we only had a sail," muttered the captain, with a sigh.

"Sail, cappen—lookee talpolin!" said Saloo, speaking in "pigeon English," and pointing to the tarpaulin in the bottom of the boat. "Why no him makee sail?"

"Yis, indade; why not?" questioned the Irishman.

"Comee, Multa! you help me; we step one oal —it makee mass—we lig him up little time."

"All roight, Sloo," responded Murtagh, leaning over and seizing one of the oars, while the Malay lifted the tarpaulin from where it lay folded up, and commenced shaking the creases out of it.

With the dexterity of a practised sailor, Murtagh soon had the oar upright, and its end "stepped," between two ribs of the boat, and firmly lashed to one of the strong planks that served as seats. Assisted by the captain himself, the tarpaulin was bent on, and with a "sheet" attached to one corner, rigged sail-fashion. In an instant it caught the stiff breeze, and bellied out; when the pinnace, feeling the impulse, began to move rapidly through the water, leaving in her wake a stream of sparkling phosphorescence that looked like liquid fire.

THE ALBATROSS. Page 26.

They had no compass, and therefore could not tell the exact direction in which they were being carried. But a yellowish streak on the horizon, showing where the sun had set, was still lingering when the wind began to freshen, and as it was one of those steady, regular winds, that endure for hours without change, they could by this means guess at the direction—which was toward that part of the horizon where the yellowish spot had but lately faded out; in short, toward the west.

Westward from the place where the cyclone had struck the ship, lay the great island of Borneo. They knew it to be the nearest land, and for this had they been directing the boat's course ever since their disaster. The tarpaulin now promised to bring them nearer to it in one night than their oars had done with days of hopeless exertion.

It was a long twelve-hour night; for under the "Line"—and they were less than three degrees from it—the days and nights are equal. But throughout all its hours, the wind continued to blow steadily from the same quarter; and the spread tarpaulin, thick and strong, caught every puff of it, acting admirably. It was, in fact, as much canvas as the pinnace could well have carried on such a rough sea-breeze, and served as a storm-trysail to run her before the wind.

Captain Redwood himself held charge of the tiller; and all were cheered with the fine speed they were making—their spirits rising in proportion to the distance passed over. Before daylight came to add to their cheerfulness, they must have made nearly a hundred miles; but ere the day broke, a sound fell upon their ears that caused a commotion among them—to all giving joy. It came swelling over the dark surface of the deep, louder than the rush of the water or the whistling of the wind. It resembled a human voice; and although like one speaking in agony, they heard it with joy. There was hope in the proximity of human beings, for though these might be in trouble like themselves, they could not be in so bad a state. They might be in danger from the storm; but they would be strong and healthy—not thirsting skeletons like the occupants of the pinnace.

"What do you think it is, captin?" asked the Irishman. "Moight it be some ship in disthriss?"

Before the captain could reply, the sound came a second time over the waters, with a prolonged wail, like the cry of a suffering sinner on his death-bed.

"The *dugong!*" exclaimed Saloo, this time recognizing the melancholy note, so like to the voice of a human being.

"It is," rejoined Captain Redwood. "It's that, and nothing more."

He said this in a despairing tone, for the dugong, which is the *manatee*, or the sea-cow of the Eastern seas, could be of no service to them; on the contrary, its loud wailings spoke of danger—these being the sure precursors of a storm.*

To him and Murtagh, the presence of this strange cetaceous animal gave no relief; and, after hearing its call, they sank back to their seats, relapsing into the state of half despondency, half hopefulness, from which it had startled them.

Not so with Saloo, who better understood its habits. He knew they were amphibious, and that, where the dugong was found, land could not be a long way off. He said this, once more arousing his companions by his words to renewed expectancy.

The morning soon after broke, and they beheld boldly outlined against the fast-clearing sky the blue mountains of Borneo.

"Land!" was the cry that came simultaneously from their lips.

---

* We are unwilling to interrupt the course of our narrative by disquisitions on subjects of natural history, and, therefore, relegate to a note the following particulars about the dugong. This strange mammal belongs to a genus of the family *Manatidæ*, or Herbivorous Cetacea. The species of which a member was discovered by our castaways, is the *Halicore Indicus*, or dugong of the Indian Archipelago; and, as we have said, is never found very far from land. Its dentition resembles, in some respects, that of the elephant; and from the structure of its digestible organs it can eat only vegetable food; that is, the *algæ*, or weeds, growing on submarine rocks in shallow water. When it comes to the surface to breathe, it utters a peculiar cry, like the lowing of a cow. Its length, when full grown, is said to be twenty feet, but few individuals seem to exceed twelve feet. In its general appearance it is very much like the *manatee*, or manatus, which haunts the mouths of the great South American rivers.

"Land—thank the Lord!" continued the American skipper, in a tone of pious gratitude; and as his pinnace, still obedient to the breeze and spread tarpaulin, forged on toward it, he once more knelt down in the bottom of the boat, caused his children to do the same, and offered up a prayer—a fervent thanksgiving to the God alike of land and sea, who was about to deliver him and his from the "dangers of the deep."

CHAPTER V.

RUNNING THE BREAKERS.

THE Almighty Hand that had thus far helped the castaways on their course, with a favoring wind bringing them in sight of Borneo's isle, was not going to crush the sweet hopes thus raised by wrecking their boat upon its shores.

And yet for a time it seemed as if this were to be their fate. As they drew near enough to the land to distinguish its configuration, they saw a white line like a snow-wreath running between it and them, for miles to right and left, far as the eye could reach. They knew it to be a barrier of coral breakers, such as usually encircle the islands of the Indian seas—strong ramparts raised by tiny insect creatures, to guard these fair gardens of God against the assaults of an ocean that, although customarily calm, is at times aroused by the *typhoon*, until it rages around them with dark scowling waves, like battalions of demons.

On drawing near these reefs, Captain Redwood, with the eye of an experienced seaman, saw that while the wind kept up there was no chance for the pinnace to pass them; and to run head on to them would be simply to dash upon destruction. Sail was at once taken in, by letting go the sheet, and dropping the tarpaulin back into the bottom of the boat. The oar that had been set up as a mast was left standing, for there were five others lying idle in the pinnace; and with four of these, Saloo and Murtagh each taking a pair, the boat was manned, the captain himself keeping charge of the tiller. His object was not to approach the land, but to prevent being carried among the breakers, which, surging up snow-white, presented a perilous barrier to their advance.

To keep the boat from driving on the dangerous reef, was just as much as the oarsmen could accomplish. Weakened as they were, by long suffering and starvation, they had a tough struggle to hold the pinnace as it were in *statu quo* — all the tougher from the disproportion between such a heavy craft and the light oar-stroke of which her reduced and exhausted crew were capable.

But as if taking pity upon them, and in sympathy with their efforts, the sun, as he rose above the horizon, seemed to smile upon them and hush the storm into silence. The wind, that throughout the night had been whistling in their ears, all at once fell to a calm, as if commanded by the majestic orb of day; and along with the wind went down the waves, the latter subsiding more gradually. It was easier now to hold the pinnace in place, as also to row her in a direction parallel to the line of the breakers; and, after coasting for about a mile, an opening was at length observed where the dangerous reef might perhaps be penetrated with safety.

Setting the boat's head toward it, the oars were once more worked with the utmost strength that remained in the arms of the rowers, while her course was directed with all the skill of which an American skipper is capable.

Yet the attempt was one of exceeding peril. Though the wind had subsided, the swell was tremendous; billow after billow being carried against the coral reefs with a violence known only to the earthquake and the angry ocean. Vast volumes of water surged high on either side, projecting still higher their sparkling shafts of spray, like the pillars of a waterspout.

Between them spread a narrow space of calm sea—yet only comparatively calm, for even there an ordinary boat, well managed, would be in danger of getting swamped. What then was the chance for a huge pinnace, poorly manned, and therefore sure of being badly trimmed? It looked as if after all the advantages that had arisen—that had sprung up as though providentially in their favor—Captain Redwood and the small surviving remnant of his crew were to perish among the breakers of Borneo, and be devoured by the ravenous sharks which amidst the storm-vexed reefs find their congenial home.

But it was not so to be. The prayer offered up, as those snow-white but treacherous perils first hove in sight, had been heard on high; and He who had guided the castaways to the danger, stayed by their side, and gave strength to their arms to carry them through it.

With a skill drawn from the combination of clear intelligence and long experience, Captain Redwood set the head of his pinnace straight for the narrow and dangerous passage; and with a strength inspired by the peril, Murtagh and the Malay pulled upon their oars, each handling his respective pair as if his life depended on the effort.

With the united will of oarsmen and steerer the effort was successful; and ten seconds later the pinnace was safe inside the breakers, moving along under the impulse of two pairs of oars, that rose and fell as gently as if they were pulling her over the surface of some placid lake.

In less than ten minutes her keel touched bottom

on the sands of Borneo, and her crew, staggering ashore, dropped upon their knees, and in words earnest as those uttered by Columbus at Cat Island, or the Pilgrims on Plymouth Rock, breathed a d vout thanksgiving for their deliverance.

CHAPTER VI.

A GIGANTIC OYSTER.

"ATER! water!"
The pain of hunger is among the hardest to endure, though there is still a harder—that of thirst. In the first hours of either, it is doubtful which of the two kinds of suffering is the more severe; but, prolonged beyond a certain point, hunger loses its keenness of edge, through the sheer weakness of the sufferer, while the agony of thirst knows no such relief.

Suffering, as our castaways were, from want of food for nearly a week, their thirst was yet more agonizing; and after the thanksgiving prayer had passed from their lips, their first thought was of water—their cry, "Water! water!"

As they arose to their feet they instinctively looked around to see if any brook or spring were near.

An ocean was flowing beside them; but this was not the kind of water wanted. They had already had enough of the briny element, and did not even turn their eyes upon it. It was landward they looked; scanning the edge of the forest, that came down within a hundred yards of the shore—the strip of sand on which they had beached their boat trending along between the woods and the tidewater as far as the eye could trace it. A short distance off, however, a break was discernible in the line of the sand-strip—which they supposed must be either a little inlet of the sea itself, or the outflow of a stream If the latter, then were they fortunate indeed.

Saloo, the most active of the party, hastened toward it; the others following him only with their eyes.

They watched him with eager gaze, trembling between hope and fear—Captain Redwood more apprehensive than the rest. He knew that in this part of the Bornean coast months often pass without a single shower of rain; and if no stream or spring should be found they would still be in danger of perishing by thirst.

They saw Saloo bend by the edge of the inlet, scoop up some water in his palms, and apply it to his lips, as if tasting it. Only for an instant, when back to them came the joyful cry,—

"*Ayer! ayer manis! süngi!*" (Water! sweet water! A river!)

Scarce more pleasantly, that morning at daybreak, had fallen on their ears the cry of "Land!" than now fell the announcement of the Malay sailor, making known the proximity of water. Captain Redwood, who was acquainted with the Malay language, translated the welcome words. Sweet water, Saloo had described it. Emphatically might it be so termed.

All hastened, or rather rushed, toward the stream, fell prostrate on their faces by its edge, and drank to a surfeit. It gave them new life; and, indeed, it had given them their lives already, though they knew it not. It was the outflow of its current into the ocean that caused the break in the coral reef through which their boat had been enabled to pass. Otherwise they might have found no opening, and perished in attempting to traverse the surging surf. The madrepores will not build their subaqueous coral walls where rivers run into the ocean; hence the open spaces here and there happily left, that form deep transverse channels admitting the largest ships.

No longer suffering from thirst, its kindred appetite now returned with undivided agony, and the next thought was for something to eat.

They again turned their eyes toward the forest, and up the bank of the stream that came flowing from it. But Saloo had seen something in the sea, near the spot where the pinnace had been left; and, calling upon Murtagh to get ready some dry wood and kindle a fire, he ran back toward the boat.

Murtagh, the rest accompanying him, walked to the edge of the woods where the stream issued from the leafy wilderness.

Just beyond the strip of sand the forest abruptly ended, the trees standing thick together, and rising like a vast vegetable wall to a height of over a hundred feet. Only a few straggled beyond this line. The very first of them, that nearest the sea, was a large elm-like tree, with tall trunk, and spreading leafy limbs that formed a screen from the sun, now well up in the sky, and every moment growing more sultry. It offered a convenient camping-place; and under its cool shadow they could recline until with restored strength they might either seek or build themselves a better habitation.

An ample store of dry faggots was lying near; and Murtagh having collected them into a pile, took out his flint and steel, and commenced striking a light.

Meanwhile their eyes were almost constantly turned toward Saloo, all of them wondering what had taken him back to the boat. Their wonder was not diminished when they saw him pass the place where the pinnace had been pulled up on the sand, and wade straight out into the water—as if he were going back to the breakers!

Presently, after he had got about knee-deep, they saw him stoop down, until his body was nearly buried under the sea, and commence what appeared to be a struggle with some creature still concealed from their observation. Nor was their wonder any the less, when at length he rose erect again, holding in his hands what for all the world looked like a huge rock, to which a number of small shells and some sea-weed adhered.

"What does the Malay crather want wid a big stone?" was the interrogatory of the astonished Irishman. "And, look, captin, it's that same he's about bringin' us. I thought it moight be some kind of shill-fish. Hungry as we are, we can't ate stones!"

"Not so fast, Murtagh," said the captain, who had more carefully scrutinized the article Saloo had taken up. "It's not a stone, but what you first supposed it—a shell-fish."

"That big thing a shill-fish! Arrah now, captin, aren't you jokin'?"

"No, indeed. What Saloo has got in his arms, if I'm not mistaken, is an oyster."

"An oysther? Two fut in length and over one in breadth. Why, it's as much as the Malay can carry. Don't yez see that he's staggerin' under it?"

"Very true; but it's an oyster for all that. I'm now sure of it, as I can see its shape, and the great ribs running over it. Make haste, and get your fire kindled; for it's a sort of oyster rather too strong-flavored to be eaten raw. Saloo evidently intends it to be roasted."

Murtagh did as requested, and by the time the Malay, bearing his heavy burden, reached the tree, smoke was oozing through a stack of faggots that were soon after ablaze.

"Tha, Cappen Ledwud," said the Malay, flinging his load at the captain's feet. "Tha plenty shell-fiss—makee all we big blakfass. Inside find good meat. We no need open him. Hot coalee do that."

They all gathered around the huge shell, surveying it with curiosity, more especially the young people.

It was that strange testaceous fish found in the Indian seas, and known to sailors as the "Singapore oyster"—of which specimens are not rare measuring a yard in length, and over eighteen inches in breadth at the widest diameter.

Their curiosity, however, was soon satisfied; for with stomachs craving as theirs, they were in no very fit condition for the pursuit of conchological studies; and Saloo once more lifting the large oyster—just as much as he could do—dropped it among the faggots, now fairly kindled into a fire.

More were heaped around and over it, until it was buried in the heart of a huge pile, the seaweeds that still clung to it crackling, and the salt water spurting and spitting, as the smoke, mingled with the bright blaze, ascended toward the overshadowing branches of the tree.

In due time Saloo, who had cooked Singapore oysters before, pronounced it sufficiently roasted; when the faggots were kicked aside, and with a boat-hook, which Murtagh had brought from the pinnace, the oyster* was dragged out of the ashes.

Almost instantly it fell open, its huge valves displaying in their concave cups enough " oyster meat" to have afforded a supper for a party of fifteen individuals instead of five—that is, fifteen not so famished as they were.

With some knives and other utensils, which the Irishman had also brought away from the boat, they seated themselves around the grand bivalve; nor did they arise from their seats until the shells were scraped clean, and hunger, that had so long tortured them, was quite banished from their thoughts.

* Strictly speaking, the Singapore oyster is a gigantic species of Clam Tridacna).

CHAPTER VII.

A DANGEROUS LOCALITY.

AFTER their ample meal of oyster "roasted in the shell," which was a breakfast instead of a supper, they rested for the remainder of the day, and all through the following night. They required this lengthened period of repose, not because they stood in need of sleep, but from the exhaustion of weakness, consequent upon their long spell of hunger and thirst.

They slept well, considering that they had no couch, nor any covering, but the tattered clothes they wore upon their bodies. But they had become accustomed to this kind of bed; as to one even less comfortable, and certainly not safer—on the hard planks of the pinnace. Nor did the cold discomfort them; for although the nights are colder on land than at sea, and in the tropics sometimes even chilly, that night was warm throughout; and nothing interfered with their slumbers except some horrid dreams, the sure sequence of suffering and perils such as they had been passing through.

The morning rose bright and beautiful, as nearly all Bornean mornings do. And the castaways rose from their recumbent position, feeling wonderfully restored both in strength and spirits. Henry and Helen—these were the names of the young people —were even cheerful, inclined to wander about and wonder at the strange objects around; the beautiful beach of silvery sand; the deep blue sea; the white breakers beyond, rising over it like a long snow-wreath; the clear fresh-water stream alongside, in which they could see curious fish disporting themselves; the grand forest-trees, among them stately palms and tall lance-like bamboos;—in short, a thousand things that make tropical scenery so charming.

Notwithstanding the scenic beauty, there was something needed before it could be thoroughly enjoyed, and this was breakfast. The contents of the great oyster had given full satisfaction for the time; but that was nearly twenty-four hours ago, and the appetites of all were once more keenly whetted. What was to take the edge off them? This was the question that occupied their thoughts, and the answer was not so easy.

Saloo went in search of another Singapore oyster; Murtagh started along the bank of the stream, in the hope of beguiling some of the red and gold fish he saw playing "backgammon" in it, as he had seen the trout and salmon in his native Killarney; while the captain, having procured a rifle, that had been brought away in the boat, and which he well knew how to handle, wandered off into the woods.

Henry and Helen remained under the tree, as their father did not think there could be any danger in leaving them alone. He was well enough acquainted with the natural history of Borneo to know that there were neither lions nor tigers in the island. Had it been on the neighboring island of Sumatra, or some desert coast of the mainland—in Malacca, Cochin China, or Hindustan—he might have dreaded exposing them to the attack of tigers. But as there was no danger of encountering these fierce creatures on the shores of Borneo, he told the children to stay under the tree until he and the others should return.

The young people were by this time rather tired of remaining in a recumbent position. It was that to which they had been too long constrained while in the boat, and it felt irksome; moreover, the oyster, wonderfully restoring their strength, had brought back their wonted juvenile vigor, so that they felt inclined for moving about a bit. For a time they indulged this inclination by walking to and fro around the trunk of the tree.

Soon, however, weariness once more came upon them, and they desired to have a seat. Squatting upon the ground is an attitude only easy to savages, and always irksome to those accustomed to habits of civilized life, and to sitting upon chairs. They looked about for something upon which they might sit, but nothing appeared suitable. There were neither logs nor large stones; for the beach, as well as the adjacent shore, was composed of fine drift-sand, and no trees seemed to have fallen near the spot.

"I have it!" exclaimed Henry, after puzzling his brains a bit, his eye guiding him to a settlement of the difficulty. "The shells—the big oyster shells—the very things for us to sit upon, sister Nell."

As he spoke, he stooped down and commenced turning over one of the shells of the immense bivalve—both of which had been hitherto lying with their concave side uppermost. It was nigh as much as the boy, still weak, could do to roll it over, though Helen, seeing the difficulty, laid hold with her little hands and assisted him.

Both the huge "cockles" were speedily capsized; and their convex surfaces rising nearly a foot above the level of the ground, gave the young people an excellent opportunity of getting seated.

Both sat down—each upon a shell—laughing at the odd kind of stools thus conveniently provided for them.

They had not been long in their sedentary attitude, when a circumstance occurred which told them how unsafe a position they had chosen. They were conversing without fear, when Henry all at once felt something strike him on the arm, and then, with a loud crash, drop down upon the shell close under his elbow, chipping a large piece out of it.

His first impression was that some one had thrown a stone at him. It had hit him on the arm, just creasing it; but on looking at the place where he had been hit, he saw that the sleeve of his jacket was split, or rather torn, from shoulder to elbow, as if a sharp-tooth currycomb had been drawn violently along it. He felt pain, moreover, and saw blood upon his shirt underneath!

He looked quickly around to ascertain who had thus rudely assailed him—anxiously, too, for he was in some dread of seeing a savage spring from the bushes close by. On turning, he at once beheld the missile that had rent his jacket-sleeve lying on the sand beside him. It was no stone, but a round or slightly oval-shaped ball, as big as a ten-pound shot, of a deep-green color, and covered all over with spurs like the skin of a hedgehog!

He at once saw that it had not been thrown at him by any person; for, with the sharp, prickly protuberances thickly set all over it, no one could have laid hand upon it. Clearly it had fallen from the tree overhead. Helen had perceived this sooner than he; for, sitting a little way off, she had seen the huge ball drop in a perpendicular direction—

though it had descended with the velocity of lightning.

Beyond doubt it was some fruit or nut from the tree under which they were seated. From the way in which the jacket-sleeve had suffered, as well as the skin underneath—to say nothing of the piece chipped out of the shell—it was evident that had the ponderous pericarp fallen upon Henry's skull, it would have crushed it as a bullet would the shell of an egg.

Young as the two were, they were not so simple as to stay in that spot an instant longer. On the tree that could send down such a dangerous missile there might be many more—equally ready to rain upon them—and with this apprehension both sprang simultaneously to their feet and rushed out into the open ground, not stopping till they believed themselves quite clear of the overshadowing branches that so ill protected them. They looked back at the seats they had so abruptly vacated, and the green globe lying beside them and then up to the tree; where they could see other similar large globes, only at such a vast height looking no bigger than peaches or apricots.

They did not dare to venture back to their seats, nor, although tempted by a strong curiosity to examine it, to approach the fallen fruit. In fact, the arm of Henry was badly lacerated; and his little sister, on seeing the blood upon his shirt-sleeve, uttered an alarm that brought first Saloo, and then the others, affrighted to the spot.

"What is it?" were the interrogations of the two white men, as they came hurrying up, while the impressive Malay put none—at once comprehending the cause of the alarm. He saw the scratched arm, and the huge green globe lying upon the ground.

"*Dulion!*" he said, glancing up to the tree.

"Durion!" echoed the captain, pronouncing the word properly, as translated from Saloo's pigeon English.

"Yes, cappen; foolee me no think of him befole. Belly big danger. It fallee on skull, skull go clashee clashee."

This was evident without Saloo's explanation. The lacerated arm and broken shell were evidences enough of the terrible effects that would have been produced had the grand pericarp in its downward descent fallen upon the heads of either of the children, and they all saw what a narrow escape Henry had of getting his "cocoa-nut" crushed or split open.

4

CHAPTER VIII.

SHOOTING AT FRUIT.

AS soon as the three men had got well up to the ground and ascertained the cause of Helen's alarm, and the damage done to Henry's jacket and skin, Murtagh was the first to make a demonstration. He did so by running in under the tree, and stooping to lay hold of the fruit that had caused the misfortune. Saloo saw him do this without giving a word of warning. He was, perhaps, a little piqued that the Irishman should make himself so conspicuous about things he could not possibly be supposed to understand, and which to the Malay himself were matters of an almost special knowledge. There was a twinkle of mischief in his eye as he contemplated the meddling of Murtagh, and waited for the *denouement*.

The latter, rashly grasping the spiny fruit, did not get it six inches above the ground, before he let go again, as if it had been the hottest of hot "purtatees."

"Och, and what have I done now!" he cried, "I'm jagged all over. There isn't a smooth spot upon it—not so much as a shank to take howlt of!"

"You takee care, Multa," cautioned Saloo. "You lookee aloft. May be you get jagee in de skull!"

Murtagh took the hint, and, giving one glance upward, ran back with a roar from under the shadow of the tree.

The Malay, seemingly satisfied with his triumph, now glided underneath the durion, and keeping his eye turned upward, as if intently watching something, he struck the fruit with the piece of pointed stick which he had been using in the search after Singapore oysters, and sent it spinning out upon the open sand beach. Then following, he took out his knife, and inserting the blade among its thickly set spines, cleft it open, displaying the pulp inside.

There was enough to give each person a taste of this most luscious of fruits, and make them desirous of more; even had they not been hungry. But the appetites of all were now keen, and neither the chase nor the fishery had produced a single thing to satisfy them. All three had returned empty-handed. There were many more nuts on the durion-tree. They could see scores of the prickly pericarps hanging overhead, but so high as to make the obtaining of them apparently impossible. They were as far away as the grapes from the fox of the fable.

The stem of the tree rose over seventy feet before throwing out a single branch. It was smooth, moreover, offering neither knot nor excrescence for a foothold. For all this Saloo could have climbed it, had he been in proper strength and condition. But he was not so. He was still weak from the effects of his suffering at sea.

Something more must be had to eat—whether game, fish, or shell-fish.

The one great oyster appeared to be astray. Saloo had begun to despair of being able to find another. The fruit of the durion proved not only pleasant eating, but exceedingly nutritious. It would sustain them, could they only get enough of it. How was this to be obtained?

For a time they stood considering; when Captain Redwood became impressed with an original idea.

In addition to his own rifle, a large ship's musket had been put into the pinnace. He thought of chain-shot, and its effects; and it occurred to him that by this means the durions might be brought down from their lofty elevation.

No sooner conceived than carried into execution. The musket was loaded with a brace of balls united by a piece of stout tarred string. A shot was fired

WHAT CAN IT BE? Page 52.

into the tree, aimed at a place where the fruit appeared thickest. There was havoc made among the adjacent leaves; and five or six of the great pericarps came crashing to the earth. A repetition of the firing brought down nearly a dozen, enough to furnish the whole party with food for at least another twenty-four hours.

Having collected the fallen pericarps, they carried them to another tree that stood near, amid whose leafy branches appeared to be no fruits either so sweet to the lips or dangerous to the skull.

Thither also they transferred their quarters, along with the paraphernalia brought up from the boat, intending to make a more permanent encampment under the newly chosen tree.

For the time they kindled no fire, as the weather was warm enough, and the durions did not require cooking; and while making their mid-day meal of the raw fruit, Saloo interested them by relating some particulars of the tree from which it had been obtained.

We shall not follow the Malay's exact words, for, as spoken in "pigeon English," they would scarce be understood; but shall lay before our readers some account of this strange and valuable fruit-tree, culled partly from Saloo's description and partly from other sources.

The durion is a forest-tree of the loftiest order, bearing resemblance to the elm, only with a smooth bark, which is also scaly. It is found growing throughout most of the islands of the Indian Archipelago; and, like the mangosteen, does not thrive well in any other part of the world. This is perhaps the reason its fruit is so little known elsewhere, as when ripe it will not bear transportation to a great distance. The fruit is nearly globe-shaped, though a little oval, and in size equals the largest cocoa-nut.

As the reader already knows, it is of a green color, and covered with short stout spines, very sharp pointed, whose bases touch each other, and are consequently somewhat hexagonal in shape. With this *chevaux-de-frise* it is so completely armed, that when the stalk is broken close off it is impossible to take up the fruit without having one's fingers badly pricked. The outer rind is tough and strong, that no matter from what height the fruit fall it is never crushed or broken. From the base of the fruit to its apex, five faint lines may be traced running among the spines. These form the divisions of the carpels, where the fruit can be cut open with a sharp knife, though requiring a considerable exertion of strength. The five cells found within are of a silken white color, each filled with an oval-shaped mass of cream-colored pulp containing several seeds of the size of chestnuts. The pulp forms the edible portion of the fruit, and its consistence and flavor are both difficult to be described. Mr. Wallace, the celebrated hunter naturalist, thus quaintly describes it:

"A rich, butter-like custard, highly flavored with almonds, gives the best general idea of it; but intermingled with it come wafts of flavor that call to mind cream-cheese, onion-sauce, brown-sherry, and other incongruities. Then there is a rich glutinous smoothness in the pulp, which nothing else possesses, but which adds to its delicacy. It is neither acid, nor sweet, nor juicy; yet one feels the want of none of these qualities, for it is perfect as it is. It produces no nausea, or other bad effects; and the more you eat of it the less you feel inclined to stop. In fact, to eat durions is a new sensation, worth a voyage to the East to experience. When the fruit is ripe it falls of itself; and the only way to eat durions to perfection is to get them as they fall, and the smell is then less overpowering. When unripe, it makes a very good vegetable if cooked, and it is also eaten by the Dyaks raw. In a good fruit season large quantities are preserved salted, in jars and bamboos, and kept the year round, when it acquires a most disgusting odor to Europeans, but the Dyaks appreciate it highly as a relish with their rice. There are in the forest two varieties of wild durions with much smaller fruits, one of them orange-colored inside. It would not perhaps be correct to say that the durion is the best of all fruits, because it cannot supply the place of a sub-acid juicy kind, such as the orange, grape, mango, and mangosteen, whose refreshing and cooling qualities are so wholesome and grateful; but as producing a food of the most exquisite flavor, it is unsurpassed. If I had to fix on two only as representing the perfection of the two classes, I should certainly choose the durion and the orange as the king and queen of fruits.

"The durion is however sometimes dangerous. When the fruit begins to ripen it falls daily and almost hourly, and accidents not unfrequently happen to persons walking or working under the trees. When the durion strikes a man in its fall it produces a dreadful wound, the strong spines tearing open the flesh, whilst the blow itself is very heavy; but from this very circumstance death rarely ensues, the copious effusion of blood preventing the inflammation which might otherwise take place. A Dyak chief informed me that he had been struck by a durion falling on his head, which he thought would certainly have caused his death, yet he recovered in a very short time."

Both the natives of the Malayan Archipelago and strangers residing there regard the durion as superior to all other kinds of fruit—in short, the finest in the world. The old traveller, Luischott, writing of it as early as 1599, says that in flavor it surpasses all other fruits. While another old traveller, Doctor Paludanus, thus speaks of it:

"This fruit is of a hot and humid nature. To those not used to it, it seems at first to smell like rotten onions, but immediately they have tasted it they prefer it to all other food. The natives give it honorable titles, exalt it, and make verses on it." *

* To these particulars we may add that the durion (*Durio zibethinus*) belongs to the natural family of *Sterculiaceæ*, of the same sub-order (*Bombaceæ*) as the silk-cotton tree. It grows to a great stature; its leaves are like those of the cherry, and its pale yellow flowers hang in large bunches. Each tree yields about two hundred fruit in a year. The fruit contains ten to twelve seeds, as large as pigeons eggs, and these, when roasted, are as good as, and taste very much like, roasted chestnuts.

CHAPTER IX.

GAGGING A GAVIAL.

AFTER finishing their dinner of durions the three men again sallied forth to see whether something more substantial could be found for a later repast— either flesh, fowl, or fish. As before, they went in different directions—Captain Redwood into the forest, Murtagh up the stream, and Saloo along the sea-beach, where he waded out into the water, still in the hope of picking up another large oyster. He took with him a stalk of bamboo, pointed at one end, to be used as a probe in the soft bottom in case any oysters might be lying *perdu* beneath the sand.

Henry and Helen were again left to themselves, but this time they were not to remain seated under any tree—at least not all the time. The father, before leaving, had enjoined upon both of them to take a bath; ablution having become very necessary on account of their having been so long cribbed up in the somewhat dirty pinnace. It would be also of service in promoting their restoration to health and strength. They went into the water, not together, but at some distant apart—Henry choosing to go down to the sea, while Helen entered the stream close by, as it had clear water with a smooth, sandy bed; besides, she thought it was safer, being free from surf or currents.

It was only safer in appearance, as the sequel proved; for the hunters and fisherman had scarce scattered off out of hearing, when a cry broke upon the still air of noon that startled the bright-winged birds of the Bornean forest, and stopped their songs as quickly as would have done a shot from Captain Redwood's rifle. It was heard by the captain himself, strolling among the tree trunks, and looking aloft for game; by Murtagh on the river bank, endeavoring to beguile the sly fish to his baited hook; by Saloo, wading knee-deep in search of Singapore oysters; and by Henry swimming about upon the buoyant incoming tide. More distinctly than all the rest, the little Helen heard it—since it was she who gave it utterance.

It was a cry of distress, and brought all the others together, and running toward the point whence it came. There was no difficulty about their knowing the direction, for one and all recognized Helen's voice, and knew where she had been left.

In less than sixty seconds' time they stood

together upon the bank of the stream, on the same spot from which they had parted; and there beheld a spectacle that thrilled them with fear, and filled them with horror.

The girl, finding it not deep enough by the edge of the stream—at this point nearly a hundred yards in width—had waded midway across, where it came quite up to her neck; and there she stood, her head alone showing above the surface. Beyond her, and coming from the opposite side, showed another head, so hideous it was no wonder that, on first perceiving it, she had given way to affright, and voice to her terror.

It was the head of an enormous reptile, of lizard shape, that had crawled out from a reedy covert on the opposite side of the river, and having silently let itself down into the water, was now swimming toward the terrified bather. There could be no mistaking the monster's intent, for it was coming straight toward its victim.

"*A gavial!*" cried Saloo, as his eyes rested on the body of the huge saurian, full twenty feet in length, with its head over a yard long, and jaws nearly the same, the upper one surmounted by a long knob-like protuberance, that distinguishes it from all other reptiles.

"A gavial!" echoed the others, though not inquiringly; for they knew too well both the shape and character of the creature that was crossing the river.

As all four first reached the bank—arriving nearly at the same instant of time—there were about twenty yards between the hideous saurian and her who seemed destined to destruction. On first perceiving her danger, the girl had made a few plunges to get back to the bank; but, hindered by the depth to which she had unwarily waded, and overcome by terror, she had desisted from the attempt; and now stood neck-deep, giving utterance to cries of despair.

What was to be done? In less than a minute more the jaws of the saurian would close upon her, crashing her fair, tender form between its teeth as though she were only some ordinary prey—a fish, or the stem of some succulent water-plant!

Her father stood on the bank a very picture of distress. Of what use the rifle held half-raised in his hands? Its bullet, not bigger than a pea, would strike upon the skull of such a huge creature harmlessly, as a drop of hail or rain. Even could he strike it in the eye—surging through the water as it was, a thing so uncertain—that would not hinder it from the intent so near to accomplishment. The Irishman, with only fish-hooks in his hand, felt equally impotent; and what could the boy Henry do, not only unarmed but undressed—in short, just as he had been bathing—*in puris naturalibus?*

All three were willing to rush into the water,

and getting between the reptile and its victim, confront the fierce creature, even to their own certain sacrifice.

And this, one, or other, or all of them, would have done, had they not been prevented by Saloo. With a loud shout the Malay, hitherto apparently impassive, called upon them to hold back. They obeyed, seeing that he intended to act, and had already taken his measures for rescuing the girl. They could not tell what these were, and only guessed at them by what they saw in his hands. It was nothing that could be called a weapon— only a piece of bamboo, pointed at one end, which he had taken from among the embers of last night's fire and sharpened with his knife, when he went off in search of the Singapore oysters. It was the same stick he had been using to probe for them under the sand. On seeing the gavial as it started toward the girl, he had quickly drawn out his knife, and sharpened the other end of the stake while coming across the beach.

With this sorry apology for a weapon, and while they were still wondering, he dashed into the stream; and almost before any of the others had recovered from their first surprise, they saw him plunge past the spot where stood the affrighted girl. In another instant his black head, with the long dark hair trailing behind it, appeared in close juxtaposition to the opened jaws of the reptile.

Then the head was seen suddenly to duck beneath the surface, while at the same time a brown-skinned arm and hand rose above it with a pointed stake in its grasp—like the emblematic representation seen upon some ancient crest. Then was seen an adroit turning of the stick, so quick as to be scarce perceptible—immediately followed by a backward spring upon the part of the lizard, with a series of writhings and contortions, in which both its body and tail took part, till the water around it was lashed into foam.

In the midst of this commotion, the head of the Malay once more appeared above the surface, close to that of the girl; who, under the guidance of her strangely-skilled and truly courageous rescuer, was conducted to the bank, and delivered safe into her father's arms: stretched open to embrace her.

It was some time, however, before the stream recovered its wonted tranquillity. For nearly half an hour the struggles of the great saurian continued, its tail lashing the water into foam, as through its gagged jaws a stream rushed constantly down its throat, causing suffocation. But, in spite of its amphibious nature, drowning was inevitable; and soon after became an accomplished fact—the huge reptilian carcass drifting down stream, toward the all-absorbing ocean, to become food for sharks, or some other marine monster more hideous and ravenous than itself.

If, indeed, a more hideous and ravenous monster is to be found! It is sometimes called the Gangetic crocodile, but it is even uglier than either crocodile or alligator, and differs from both in several important particulars.

As, for instance, in its mouth—its jaws being curiously straight, long, and narrow; and in the shape of its head, which has straight perpendicular sides, and a quadrilateral upper surface. It has double, or nearly double, the number[*] of the teeth of the crocodile of the Nile, though the latter is well enough supplied with these potent implements of destruction!

It is an amphibious animal, and fond of the water, in which its webbed hind feet enable it to move with considerable celerity.

The huge reptile which threatened Helen's safety was twenty feet in length, but the gavial sometimes attains the extraordinary dimensions of eight to nine yards.

Sincere was the gratitude of Captain Redwood for the address and courage displayed by the Malay in rescuing his daughter, and his regret was great that he had no means of rewarding his faithful follower.

[*] As many as one hundred and twenty.

CHAPTER X.

BURROWING BIRDS.

THE fruit diet, however delicious, was not strengthening. Saloo said so, and Murtagh agreed with him. The Irishman declared he would rather have a meal of plain "purtatees and buttermilk," though a bit of bacon, or even ship's "junk," would be more desirable.

All agreed that a morsel of meat — whether salted or fresh — would be highly beneficial; indeed, almost necessary to the complete restoration of their strength.

How was animal food to be procured? The forest, so far as Captain Redwood had explored it, seemed altogether untenanted by living creature. He had now been tramping for upward of an hour among the trees without seeing either bird or quadruped. And although there were fish in the stream, and should have been shell-fish along the sea-beach, neither Murtagh nor Saloo had succeeded in procuring any. A keen craving for animal food had grown upon them, and they were not without some regretful thoughts at having permitted the dead gavial to drift out to sea. Even from the carcass of the saurian they might have obtained stakes that, if not very dainty or delicate, would at least have been eatable.

Discouraged by their want of success, and still feeling feeble, they did not go out again that day, but remained resting under the tree.

While they were munching their evening meal —of durions, as the dinner had been—the Malay commenced discoursing upon eggs, which set them all thinking about them. If they only had a few, it would be just the very thing to nourish and give them strength. But where were the eggs to be obtained? This was the question asked him by the Irishman, who could at that moment have eaten a dozen, boiled, fried, poached, in omelette, or even, as he said himself, have "sucked" them.

"Iggs indade!" he exclaimed, as Saloo made mention of the article; "I'd loike to see one, an' could ate a basketful of them, if they were as big as swans'. What puts iggs in your head, nigger?"

"Eggs no long way off," rejoined the Malay. "Plenty egg if we knowee whale find 'em."

"How do you know that? Ye're ravin', Saloo."

"No lavin, Multa. You heal lass night the malee? All night longee he cly wail."

"Hear the malee. What's that?"

"Biggee fowl like tulkey. Saloo heal him. Make moan likee man go die."

"Och, thair was that, thrue enough. I heerd something scramin' all the night. I thought it might be a banshee*, if thair is that crayther in this counthry. A bird, you say? What of that? Its squalling won't give us any iggs, nor lade to its nest nayther."

"Ness not belly fal way. Malee make ness in sand close to sea-shole. Mollow monin' I go lookee, maybe findee."

All throughout the previous night they had heard a voice resounding along the shore in loud, plaintive wailings, and Captain Redwood had remarked its being a strange note to him, never having heard the like before. He believed the cries to come from some species of sea-fowl that frequented the coast, but did not think of the probabilty of their nests being close at hand. As day broke he had looked out for them in hopes of getting a shot. Even had they been gulls, he would have been glad of one or two for breakfast. But there were no birds in sight, not even gulls.

Saloo now told them that the screams heard

---

* The Banshee, or Benshie, sometimes called the Shrieking Woman, is an imaginary being, supposed by the Irish to predict, by her shrieks and wails, the death of some member in the family over which she exercises a kind of supervision. To this fable Moore alludes in one of his songs—
"How oft has the Benshee cried."

during the night did not come from sea-fowl, but from birds of a very different kind, that had their home in the forest, and only came to the sea-coast during their season of breeding; that their presence was for this purpose, and therefore denoted the proximity of their nests.

While they were yet speaking on the subject, their eyes were suddenly attracted to a number of the very birds about which they were in converse. There was quite a flock of them—nearly fifty in all. They were not roosted upon the trees, nor flying through the air, but stepping along the sandy beach with a sedate yet stately tread, just like barn-door fowl on their march toward a field of freshly-sown grain, here and there stooping to pick up some stray seed. They were about the size of Cochin-Chinas, and from their flecked plumage of glossy black and rose-tinted white color, as well as from having a combed or helmeted head, and carrying their tails upright, they bore a very striking resemblance to a flock of common hens.

They, in fact, belonged to an order of birds closely allied to the gallinaceous tribe, and representing it on the continent of Australia as also in several of the Austro-Malayan islands, where the true gallinaceæ do not exist. There are several distinct species of them; some, as the *tallegalla* or "brush turkey" of Australia, approaching in form and general appearance to the turkey, while others resemble the common fowl, and still others might be regarded as a species of pheasant. They have the singular habit of depositing their eggs in mounds of rubbish, which they scrape together for this purpose, and then leave them to what might appear a sort of spontaneous incubation. Hence they are usually called "mound-builders," though they do not all adhere to the habit; some of them choosing a very different though somewhat analogous mode of getting their eggs hatched. Naturalists have given them the name of *megapoda*, on account of their very large feet, which, provided with long curved claws, enable them to scratch the ground deeply and rake together the rubbish into heaps for the safe deposit of their eggs.

Sometimes these megapodes, as the Australians call them, for they are as common in Australia as Borneo, raise heaps of fifteen feet in height, and not less than sixty feet in circumference at the base.

They are large and heavy birds, unwieldy in their motions, slow and lumbering in their flight. Their legs are thick, and their toes are also thick and long.

There is some difference between their nest-building ways and those of the tallegalla; yet, on the whole, the similarity is very striking, as may be seen from the following account.

Tracing a circle of considerable radius, says Mr.

Wood, the birds begin to travel round it, continually grasping with their large feet the leaves, and grasses, and dead twigs which are lying about, and flinging them inward toward the centre. Each time they finish their rounds they narrow their circle, so that they soon clear away a large circular belt, having in its centre a low, irregular heap. By repeating the operation they decrease the *diameter* of the mound while increasing its *height*, until at length a large and rudely conical mound is formed.

Next they scrape out a cavity of about four feet in the middle of the heap, and here deposit the eggs, which are afterward covered up, to be hatched by the combined effects of fermentation and the sun. But the bird does not thus escape any of the cares of maternity, for the male watches the eggs carefully, being endowed with a wonderful instinct which tells him the temperature suitable for them. Sometimes he covers them thickly with leaves, and sometimes lays them nearly bare, repeating these operations frequently in the course of a single day.

The eggs at last are hatched, but when the young bird escapes from the shell it does not leave the mound, remaining therein for at least twelve hours. Even after a stroll in the open air it withdraws to its mound toward evening, and is covered up, like the egg, only not to so great a depth. It is a singular fact that in all cases a nearly cylindrical hole, or shaft, is preserved in the centre of the heap, obviously intended to admit the cooling air from without, and to allow of the escape of the gases fermenting within.

In each nest as much as a bushel of eggs is frequently deposited. As these are of excellent flavor, they are quite as much esteemed by the white man as by the aborigine. The tallegalla has a habit of scratching large holes in the ground while dusting itself, says Mr. Wood, after the manner of gallinaceous birds; and these holes often serve to guide the egg-hunter toward the nest itself.

After this digression let us return to the megapodes of Borneo, whose appearance had strongly excited the curiosity of Captain Redwood and his party.

The birds that had now displayed themselves to the eyes of our party of castaways were of the species known as "maleos," by Saloo called malee. They had not just then alighted, but came suddenly into view around the spur of a "dune," or sand-hill, which up to that moment had hindered them from being observed.

As the spectators were quietly reclining under the obscure shadow of the tree, the birds did not notice them, but stalked along the shore about their own business.

What this business was soon became apparent

for although one or another of the birds made occasional stop to pick up some worm, weed, or seed, it was evident they were not making their evening promenade in search of food. Now and again one would dart quickly away from the flock, running with the swiftness of a pheasant, then suddenly stop, survey the ground in every direction, as if submitting it to examination, and finally, with a cackling note, summon the others to its side. After this a general cackle would spring up, as if they were engaged in some consultation that equally regarded the welfare of all.

It was noticed that those taking the initiative in these prospecting rushes and summonings, differed a little from the others. The casque or bonnet-shaped protuberance at the back of their heads was larger, as were also the tubercles at their nostrils; the red upon their naked cheeks was of brighter and deeper hue; while their plumage was gayer and more glossy, the rufous-white portion of it being of a more pronounced rose or salmon color. These were the male birds or "cocks" of the flock, though the difference between them and the hens was much less than that between chanticleer and the ladies of his barn-yard harem, and only noticeable when they drew very near to the spectators.

They were still two hundred yards from the spot where the latter lay watching them, and by the direction in which they were going it was not likely they would come any nearer. Captain Redwood had taken hold of the musket, intending to load it with some slugs he chanced to have, and try a long shot into the middle of the flock; but Saloo restrained him with a word or two spoken in a whisper. They were,—

"Don't try shot, cappen. Too long way off. You miss all. Maybe they go lookee place for billy eggs. Much betta we waitee while."

Thus cautioned, the captain laid aside the gun, while they all remained silently watching the maleos, which continued their course, with its various divergences, still unconscious of being observed.

When they were nearly in front of the camping-place, at a spot where the sand lay loose and dry, above the reach of the ordinary tidal influx, all made a stop at the summons of one who, from the superior style of his plumage and the greater grandeur of his strut, appeared a very important individual of the tribe—in all likelihood the "cock of the walk."

Here a much longer period was spent in the cackling consultation, which at length came to an end, not as before in their passing on to another place, but by the whole flock setting to, and with their great clawed feet scratching up the sand, which they scattered in clouds and showers all around them.

For a time they were scarce visible, the sand dust flying in every direction, and concealing the greater portion of them beneath its dun cloud; and this sort of play was continued for nearly half an hour. It was not intended for play, however, for when it at length came to a termination the spectators under the tree could perceive that a large cavity had been hollowed out in the sand, of such extent, as to diameter and depth, that more than half the flock, when within its circumference, were invisible from their point of observation.

From that moment it could be noted that several birds were always down in the pit thus excavated, some going in, others coming out, as if taking their turn in the performance of a common duty; and it was further noticed that the ones so occupied were those of less conspicuous plumage—in fact the hens; while the cocks strutted around, with their tails elevated high in the air, and with all the pride and importance usually assumed by masters of a grand ceremonial.

For another hour this singular scene was kept up, Saloo hindering his companions from making any movement to interrupt it, by promising them a great reward for non-interference.

The scene at length terminated in another grand scraping match, by which the sand was flung back into the pit with the accompanying storm of dust, and then emerging from the cloud there commenced a general stampede of the megapodes, the birds separating into parties of two and three, and going in different directions. They rushed away at lightning speed, some along the smooth sand beach, while others rose right up into the air, and on loud whirring wings flew off into the forest.

"Now!" said Saloo, with joy gleaming in his dark, Oriental eyes. "Now we gettee pay for patient waitee—we hab egg—better than dulion— belly bess solt of egg malee."

As there was no need for further concealment or caution, all started to their feet and hastened out to the spot where the departed fowls had been at work. There was no longer any signs of a hollow, but a level surface corresponding with that around, and but for the fresh look of the recently disturbed sand, and the scoring that told of claws having disturbed it, no one could have thought that a flock of birds resembling barn-door fowl had just made such a large cavity in the ground, and then filled it up again.

Saloo and Murtagh ran down to the pinnace, and each brought back an oar. With these used as shovels, the loose sand was once more removed, and nearly three dozen large eggs of a reddish or brick color were exposed to view, lying in a sort of irregular stratification. They were of the usual ovoid form, smaller at one end than the other, though but slightly elongated. What was most notable was their immense size, considering the bulk of the birds that voided them; for while the latter were not larger than common hens, the eggs were as big as those of a goose. The contents of one which Murtagh, in his careless Hibernian way, accidentally broke—and which were caught in a tin pannikin that held as much as a good-sized breakfast cup—filled the pannikin to its brim.

It was quite a seasonable supply. These fine eggs proved not inferior to those of the common hen; indeed they were thought superior, and in flavor more like the eggs of a guinea-fowl or turkey.

About a dozen of them were cooked for breakfast, and in more ways than one. Some were boiled, one of the half shells of the same Singapore oyster serving for a saucepan; while in the other, used as a frying-pan, an immense omelette was frittered to perfection. It was quite a change from the fruit diet of the durion, reversing our present as well as the old Roman fashion of eating, though not contrary to the custom of some modern nations—the Spaniards, for example. Instead of being *ab ovo ad malum*, it was *ab malo ad ovum*.*

---

* The Romans began their noonday meal with eggs, and ended with a dessert (*ab ovo ad malum*).

CHAPTER XI.

THE LANOONS.

CERTAINLY the most nutritious of all things eatable or drinkable is the substance, or fluid, called milk. It becomes blood almost immediately, and then flesh, or muscle, as was designed by the Creator. Hence it is the first food given to all animated creatures —not alone to the *mammalia*, but to the oviparous animals—even to the infantile forms of the vegetable itself. To the first it is presented in the form of simple milk, or "lacteal fluid;" to the second in the "white" of the egg; while the young tree or plant, springing from its embryo, finds it in the farina, or succulent matter, with which it is surrounded, and in which it has hitherto lain embedded and apparently lifeless, till the nursing sun calls it into a growing existence. It is albumen, gluten, and other substances combined, all existing in the udder, in the egg-shell, in the seed, root, or fruit; from which springs the progeny, whether it be man or beast, flying bird or swimming fish, creeping reptile or fast-rooted forest tree.

The meal of oyster-meat had restored to healthy action the long-fasting stomachs of the castaways; the durion fruit, coming like a *dessert*, had no doubt acted with an exceedingly beneficial effect; but not till they had partaken of the true "staff of life"—represented in one of its elementary forms, the egg—did they feel their blood running in its right channels, alike restoring their vigor and strength.

Murtagh was one of the first to feel revivified, and declare himself ready for anything. But they were all much invigorated, and began to think and talk of plans for the future. The question, of course, was, how they should quit the shore on which shipwreck, and afterward a chance wind, had cast them? So far the coast appeared to be uninhabited, and although not so very inhospitable, as their experience had proved, still it would never do for them to remain there.

The American merchant-skipper had no ambition to match the Scotchman Selkirk, and make a second Crusoe of himself. Neither would Murtagh or the Malay have cared to act as his man Friday for any very prolonged period of hermitage, so long as there was a mode of escaping from it.

During the remainder of that evening, therefore, they talked of a change of quarters, and discussed various plans for bringing this about. It was a question whether they should take to their boat and again put out to sea, or endeavor, by an overland expedition, to reach some part of the coast where they might find a European, and therefore a civilized, settlement. Captain Redwood knew there were more than one of these on the great island of Borneo. There were the Dutch residences of Sambas and Sarabang; the English government depôt on the islet of Labuan; and the strange heterogeneous settlement—half colony, half kingdom—then acknowledging the authority of the bold British adventurer, Sir James Brooke, styled "Rajah of Sarawak." If any of these places could be attained, either coastwise or across country, our castaways might consider their sufferings at an end; and it was only a question which would be the easiest to reach, and what the best way of reaching it.

After due consideration, Labuan was the point decided upon. From that part of the coast Captain Redwood supposed himself to be, it was by far the nearest civilized settlement—in fact, the only one that offered a chance of being reached by travellers circumstanced as they. Of course they had no intention to start immediately. Their strength was not sufficiently restored, and they were only discussing the question of a journey to be undertaken before long, and the probabilities of their being able to accomplish it.

Although they were now safe on land, and need no longer dread the "dangers of the deep," they did not yet believe themselves delivered from all peril. The part of the coast on which they had landed appeared uninhabited; but it was not this that made them uneasy. On the contrary, human beings were the very things they did not desire just then to see. From the place where his ship had been struck by the typhoon, and the distance and direction in which they had since drifted, Captain Redwood conjectured—was indeed almost sure of it —that they were on some part of the northeastern coast of Borneo, where it fronts the Celebes Sea; and he had traded long enough among the islands of the Malayan Archipelago to know that this was a most dangerous locality, not from beasts of prey, but fierce, predatory men; from *pirates*, in short.

These sea-robbers, issuing from their hiding-places and strongholds among the lagoons of many of the Malayan islands—more especially Mindanao —are to be met with all through the Indian Archipelago; but their most favorite cruising-grounds are in the seas lying around the Sooloo isles, and stretching between Borneo and New Guinea.

They are usually known as "Lanoons," from Illanon, the southern peninsula of Mindanao, their principal place of refuge and residence. But they have also other haunts and ports where they make rendezvous—many on the shores of the Celebes Sea, in the island of Celebes itself, and also along the eastern and northern coast of Borneo. In this last they are usually known as "Dyak pirates," a name not very correct; since most of these freebooters are of pure Malayan race, while the Bornean Dyaks take but little part in their plundering, and are themselves often its victims.

The craft in which they carry on their nefarious calling are large junk-like vessels termed "präus," with short, stumpy masts and huge square sails of woven matting stuff. But they place more dependence upon their broad paddle-bladed oars and skilled oarsmen, each präu having from thirty to forty rowers, and some very large ones a much greater number. These, seated in double rows along each side of the vessel, take no part in the fighting, which is done by the chiefs and warriors stationed above on a sort of platform or upper deck that extends nearly the whole length of the präu. The advantage derived from the oars is, that in the tropical seas very light winds and calms are of common occurrence, during either of which the präu can easily overtake an ordinary sailing-ship. And when a brisk wind arises, and it is desirable to avoid any vessel that may be endeavoring to come up with them, they can, by means of their strong rowing force, get to windward of the chasing craft, and so out of harm's way.

Ships are not always the objects of their piratical

cruisings, or they might at times find it but an unprofitable business. Combined with sea piracy, they make frequent land expeditions along the coasts of the different islands, going up the inlets and rivers, and plundering the towns or other settlements situated on their banks. And their booty does not always consist of goods, chattels, and money, but of men, women, and children; for they are men-robbers as well as murderers and pirates. Their captives are carried off to their places of rendezvous, and there kept until they can be sold into slavery—a market for this kind of commodity being easily found in almost every island of the Malayan Archipelago—whether it be Dutch, Spanish, Portuguese, or under the dominion of its own native rulers, the sultans, and rajahs.

Well aware of all these circumstances, Captain Redwood knew the danger he and his party would incur should they fall into the hands of the Lanoons. So long as they were out upon the open sea, and in fear of perishing by starvation, they had never had a thought about pirates. Then the sight of a prau—even with the certainty of its being a piratical craft—would have been welcome; since death by the Malay kris, or slavery to the most cruel taskmaster, would have been a relief from the sufferings they were enduring, from hunger as from thirst. Now, however, that these were things of the past, and they were not only safe delivered from the perils of the deep, but seemed in no farther danger of starvation, the pirates had become the subject of their gravest fears, and their eyes were habitually on the alert—now scanning the sea-shore on both sides, and now directed toward the forest, whenever any noise from that quarter occurred to excite suspicion.

While in this frame of mind, the boat which had brought them safely ashore caused them a good deal of apprehension. They might themselves have easily found concealment among the trees that stood thickly on the land-side; but the large pinnace lying upon the open beach was a conspicuous object, and could be seen miles off by any one straying along the shore, or coming abruptly out of the forest. If there were any pirates' nest near, the boat would surely betray them, and the question arose as to what should be done with it.

To have dragged it up the sand, and hidden it among the underwood, is probably what they would have done had they been possessed of sufficient strength. But they knew that they were not, and therefore the thing was not thought of. It was as much as they could yet do to drag their own bodies about, much less a heavy ship's boat.

Murtagh suggested breaking it up, and letting the fragments float off upon the waves. But Captain Redwood did not approve of this mode. The craft that had so long carried them through an un known sea, and at length set them safely ashore, deserved different treatment. Besides, they might again stand in need of it; for it was not yet certain whether they were on the coast of the Bornean mainland, or one of the numerous outlying islets to be found along its eastern side. If an island, the boat would still be required to carry them across to the main.

While they were engaged in discussing this subject on the day they had made discovery of the maleos' eggs, Saloo's sharp eye, wandering about, caught sight of something that promised a solution of the difficulty. It was the little stream not far off, or rather, the estuary formed by its current, which, flowing out through the sands, had cut a channel deep enough for the keel of a much larger craft than a ship's pinnace.

"Why we no blingee boat up libba?" he asked.

"Saloo is right; it may be done," assented the captain.

"Troth an' that may it. It's clivver of the nigger to be the first of us to think of that same. Then we'd better set about it at once—hadn't we, captin?"

"By all means," was the reply; and the three men, rising to their feet, walked off toward the boat, leaving the young people under the tree.

CHAPTER XII.

KRISSING A CONSTRICTOR.

T took them nearly an hour to get the pinnace round into the stream, and opposite the place they had fixed upon for their temporary encampment. The current acting against their feeble efforts at rowing, was the cause of delay. They succeeded, however, and the boat was made safe from being observed by the eye of any one going along the beach. But, to make it still more secure, they poled it under the branches of an overhanging tree not far off—a large Indian fig, or *banyan*, whose umbrageous top overshadowed the water nearly half-way across the stream.

To one of its numerous root-stems the craft was made fast by means of the tiller-ropes; and they were stepping out of it to return to their camping-place when a shout from Saloo warned them of some danger ahead.

It was not ahead, but *overhead ;* for, as his companions looked up—following the example of the

Malay—they saw what at first appeared to be one of the stems of the banyan in motion, as if endowed with life.

They were soon convinced of their mistake; for instead of the moving thing being part of the fig-tree, its supple, cylindrical body and glittering scales showed it to be a serpent.

It was a python, and one of enormous dimensions, as they could tell by what they saw of it, knowing that this was only a portion of the whole; at least ten feet of it were depending from the tree, while, judging by the taper of its body, and applying the ordinary rule as to serpent shape, there could not be less than ten or twelve other feet concealed among the branches above.

As Saloo first caught sight of it, it was descending from the tree, no doubt having been disturbed by the noise made in mooring the boat, and tempted to forsake its perch for some purpose unknown. It was coming down head foremost—not along any of the stems, but in an open space between them— its tail coiled round a branch above, affording it a support for this descent, monkey or 'possum-fashion.

Its snout had already touched the ground, and perhaps its whole body would soon have been elongated upon the earth but for the shout of Saloo. At this it suddenly jerked up its head, but without taking in any of its coils above; and with jaws agape and tongue protruding, it commenced oscillating around as if trying its range, and ready to pounce upon any creature that came within the radius of that wide circle of which its forked tongue was describing the circumference.

The warning of the Malay was given soon enough to save Captain Redwood, but not the ship-carpenter. Murtagh was either too long in hearing, or too slow in giving heed to it. He was a step or two in advance of the others, carrying in his arms some implements from the boat. In looking around and above he saw the snake sweeping about in its grand circular vibrations, and at the same time perceived that he was within their range.

It was but the simple obedience of instinct to leap to one side, which he did; but as ill luck would have it, hampered by the *impedimenta* carried in his arms, he came in violent collision with one of the stems of the banyan, which not only sent him back with a rebound, but threw him down upon the earth, flat on his face. He would have done better by lying still, for in that position the snake could not have coiled around and constricted him. And the python rarely takes to its teeth till it has tried its powers of squeezing.

But the ship-carpenter, ignorant of this herpetological fact, and as an Irishman not highly gifted either with patience or prudence, after scrambling a while upon his hands and knees, stood once more upon his feet.

He had scarcely got into an erect attitude when his body was embraced by a series of spiral annulations that extended from head to foot—huge thick rings, slimy and clammy to the touch, which he knew to be the foldings of the python.

Had there been any Lanoons, or Dyak pirates, within a mile's distance, they might have heard the cry that escaped him. The forest birds heard it afar off, and ceased their chatterings and warblings, so that there was no sound for some time save the continuous shrieks and ejaculations that came from Murtagh's lips.

Captain Redwood, altogether unarmed, leaped back into the pinnace to seize the boat-hook, thinking it the best weapon for the occasion. It might have been of service if obtainable in time. But long before he could have returned with it the ship-carpenter's ribs would have been compressed into a mass of broken bones, and the breath crushed out of his body.

This would certainly have been the lamentable result but for a weapon with which a Malay is always armed, carrying it on his body nearer than his shirt, and almost as near as his skin. It was the *kris*. As a matter of course, Saloo had one; and luckily for his old shipmate, "Multa," he knew how to handle it with skill, so that, in driving its twisted blade through the python's throat, he did not also impale upon its point the jugular vein of the Irishman. He did the one dexterously without doing the other, and the consequence was that the huge snake, suffering keenly from having its throat pierced through, quickly uncoiled itself from the body of its intended victim, glad to let the latter escape, and only thinking of getting free itself by scuttling off into the thickest of the underwood, where it disappeared evidently writhing in pain.

Too anxious about the condition of their comrade, neither Captain Redwood nor Saloo thought of pursuing it, but stooped down over the released body of the Irishman, who had fallen prostrate to the earth.

On due examination it proved that there was not much harm done beyond a terrible fright; and after some congratulations he was induced to get once more upon his feet and accompany them to the camp. But for Saloo and his kris, beyond doubt, he would never have returned to it alive.

For the python in the Old World is quite as formidable as the boa in the New. Perhaps it is even more to be dreaded; for, notwithstanding its great length—twenty-five to thirty feet—it is exceedingly nimble, and its muscular strength is immense. There are numerous authentic stories on record of its having crushed the buffalo and the tiger in its huge constricting folds. The *python reticulatus* is probably the largest species.

CHAPTER XIII.

CHICKS QUICK TO TAKE WING.

TWO more days passed without any occurrence of an unusual nature, though the castaways made several short excursions and explorations into the forest, and also up and down the shore, keeping, however, close to the edge of the timber. These ended without any important discovery being made, but confirmed them in their conjecture that the coast on which they had been cast was uninhabited, at least for a considerable distance on each side of the place where they had landed.

The most disappointing thing about these exploratory trips was their fruitlessness in obtaining food, the chief object for which they had been made. Excepting some stray roots and berries of an esculent nature, they had nothing to eat after the maleos' eggs were consumed; and these had lasted them only into the second day. It is true the durion stood near, and its fruit would for a time keep them from starving. Still it would do little for the restoration of their strength; and upon such diet it would be a long time before they could undertake the arduous journey contemplated with any fair prospect of being able to finish it. No more Singapore oysters could be found, no fish caught; and such birds and beasts of the forest as Captain Redwood had accidentally got a glimpse of, had either flown or fled away without giving him as much as the chance of a snap shot.

At night they again heard the stridulous clamor of the maleos, and every morning looked out for them; but these fine fowls did not put in another appearance, much less deposit three dozen eggs right under their eyes, and in a convenient spot for being gathered.

Saloo, however, who knew all about their habits, believed he might yet find another ovarium; and with this view, on the morning of the third day, after giving up all further attempts at getting shellfish, he started upon a "prospecting" expedition after eggs, the others going with him.

Their route led along the shore, and among the dry sand-wreaths, swirled up near the selvedge of the woods. If another egg depository existed, it was there it should be found. He told his companions that not only did different gangs of the maleos bury their eggs in different places, but the same tribe or flock had the habit of returning to the beach at different times, each time laying their collected eggs in a new and separate pit. That, moreover, these curious birds, guided by instinct or cunning, are accustomed to conceal the place of deposit, which might be easily recognized by their tracks and scratchings. This they do by scoring the ground in other places, and giving to the surface the same appearance as it bears over the spot where their eggs have been left to the hatching of the sun.

In this searching excursion Saloo had brought with him a boat-hook; and it was not long before he had an opportunity of proving the truth of his words. A place where the sand was very much tracked by the huge feet of the megapodes soon presented itself, exactly resembling the spot where they had procured the first supply of eggs. But on probing it with the boat-hook, Saloo at once pronounced it one of the sham nests.

After all, the creatures did not show too much cunning; for the presence of this pretended place of deposit told the Malay that a real one would not be far off; and, sure enough, another was soon after discovered, which, on being sounded by the iron point of the boat-hook, gave back a firm feel and a sharp metallic click, that told him there were eggs underneath.

The sand, as before, was carefully removed— Murtagh having brought with him an oar for the purpose—when, for the second time, nearly three dozen beautiful salmon-colored eggs were disclosed to their view.

These were carefully taken up, and carried back to the place of encampment, where they were left lying upon the ground, the party resuming their quest, in hope of being able to lay in a larger and more permanent supply.

As it chanced, another considerable receptacle was struck, giving back sweet music to the probing of the boat-hook; and its contents were also added to the larder.

As the last lot had been found under sand that appeared but recently stirred, it followed that they were fresher than those of the second finding, and therefore was it determined upon that they should be first eaten.

The egg-gatherers having been now several hours engaged, and again become almost as hungry as when first cast upon the shore, once more kindled a fire, set the huge shells upon it, and using the one as a boiling-pot, and the other as a frying-pan, prepared themselves a meal of two courses—*œuf bouille* and *omelette*.

Next day they again went in search of other eggs, intending to lay in a store against the eventuality of any possible period of famine.

But although they discovered several scratched places, and carefully "sounded" them, no more maleos' eggs could be found; and they came to the conclusion that they had despoiled all the "incubator" beds existing on that section of the Bornean coast.

By reason of their rapidly-increasing strength, their appetites were by this time almost insatiable. They were, therefore, not long in using up all the "setting" last gathered, and were about to begin upon the other lot that did not seem so "newly laid." These had been kept separate, and permitted to lie where they had first placed them—out on the open surface of the sand, some fifteen or twenty yards beyond the shadow of the tree. Negligently, and somewhat unwisely, had this been done; for during the day the hot sun shining down upon them would naturally have a tendency to spoil and addle them. Still the time had not been very long; and as no one thought of their being damaged, they were preparing to turn them into eggs poached, fried, boiled, or otherwise.

Saloo had rekindled the fire, and got ready his pots and pans; while Murtagh, who had stepped out to the "larder," was about to take up one of the eggs, and carry it to the "kitchen." But at that moment a sight met the eyes of the Irishman that not only astonished, but caused him to sing out so excitedly as at once to attract the attention of the others to the same singular spectacle.

It was that of an egg rolling, as it were, spontaneously over the ground! And not only one egg, for, as they continued to gaze a while, the whole lot, as if taking their cue from it, commenced imitating the movement, some with a gentle, others a more violent motion! Murtagh sprang back affrighted, and stood with his red hair on end, gazing at the odd and inexplicable phenomenon. The others were as much puzzled as he—all except the Malay, who at a glance understood the philosophy of the movement.

"Young malee inside," he cried in explanation. "We no eat egg, we get chickee. Wait little minnit. You him see come out full featha."

Truly enough the "chicks" did come out, not as down-covered helpless creatures, but pults in full plumage, as Saloo had predicted: at all events, full enough to enable them to fly; for as the shells one after another commenced crackling—burst outward by the young birds' strength—each showed a perfect fledgling; that, springing forth from the shivered encasement, like Jack out of his box, at once flapped its little wings, and essayed short flights over the surface of the sand.

So much were the spectators taken by surprise, that one and all of the new-born but completely equipped birds, would have winged their way into the forest and been lost, had it not been for Saloo, who, accustomed to such transformations, was in no way discomposed, but preserved his coolness and equanimity.

Fortified by these, and armed with the boat-hook, which he had suddenly seized, he struck down the precocious chicks one after another, and put an end to their aspiring flights by laying them lifeless upon the sand.

In the end it was neither eggs nor omelettes, but tender, delicate "squabs" the castaways had for their prandial repast.

CHAPTER XIV.

A GRAND TREE-CLIMBER.

THE castaways having made a repast on chicks, instead of eggs, as they had been expecting, were for the time satisfied, so far as concerned their appetites. But aware that these would ere long recommence their craving, they could not be contented to remain inactive. It would be necessary to procure some other kind of provisions, and, if possible, a permanent stock on which they could rely until ready to set out on their journey, with a surplus to carry them some way along it.

Although in Borneo there are many kinds of strange birds, and some of them large ones, they are not to be found everywhere, and when seen, not so easily caught or shot. There are some large quadrupeds too, as the Indian rhinoceros, and the Sumatran tapir; and although the flesh of these great thick-skinned animals is neither tender nor delicate, yet men who can get no other soon find themselves in a position to relish it, despite its toughness and its coarse texture. But neither rhinoceros nor tapir was seen by our castaways; neither seemed to frequent that part of the coast, as no tracks of them were observed during their excursions. If they had fallen in with a rhinoceros, they would have had some difficulty in killing it; seeing that this enormous brute is as large as a small elephant, its body protected by a thick hide, embossed with hard knob-like protuberances, like those upon shields, giving to the animal the appearance of being encased in a full suit of ancient armor.

The Sumatran tapir, too, is a creature that does not readily succumb to its assailant, being larger and stronger than its namesake of South America.

There are two species of deer known in Borneo; one of them, the "rusa," a fine large animal.

Captain Redwood was in hopes he might meet with an individual of either species; and with this object in view, he continued to make short excursions into the woods, taking his rifle along with him, occasionally accompanied by Murtagh, with the ship's musket.

But they always returned empty-handed, and a good deal down-hearted, having seen nothing that could be converted into venison.

Saloo had again tried for eggs and shell-fish, but was unsuccessful in his search after both; evidently there were no more depositories of maleos' eggs, nor Singapore oysters, nor, indeed, any kind of shell-fish, on that part of the shore. They did not again see any of the mound-making birds—not even those they had despoiled; for it is not the habit of the megapodes to return to their eggs, but to leave them to be hatched under the hot sand, and the chicks to scratch their way upward to the surface, thus taking care of themselves from the very moment of their birth, and, indeed, we may say, before it, since it can scarcely be said they are born before breaking through the shell; and this they have to do for themselves, else they would never see daylight. Talk of precocious chicks! There are none anywhere to be compared with the megapodean pullets of the Malayan Archipelago, no birds half so "early" as they.

For some days, after eating up the last chicken of the flock, our castaways could get nothing to live upon but durions; and although these formed a diet sufficiently agreeable to the palate, they were not very strengthening. Besides, they were not so easily gathered; the few they had found on some trees, which Saloo had conveniently climbed, being quickly exhausted. The large durion-tree under which they had first encamped was well furnished with fruit. But its tall stem, nearly a hundred feet, without a branch, and with a bark smooth as that of a sycamore, looked as if no mortal man could ascend it. Captain Redwood had fired several rounds of his chain-shot up into it, and brought down many of the grand spinous pericarps; but this cost an expenditure of ammunition; and, circumstanced as they were, they saw it would never do to waste it in such whimsical fashion. Still, for want of food, the fruit must be obtained some way or other, and the question was how to "pluck" it.

In their dilemma the Malay once more came to their aid. Fortunately for all, Saloo was a native of Sumatra, and had been brought up among its forests, much resembling those of Borneo. He was skilled in the wood-craft common to both islands; and, perhaps, of all the crew of the castaway ship, not one could have survived whose services would have been of more value to Captain Redwood and his party than those of the brown-skinned pilot;— especially since it had been their fate to be cast upon the shores of Borneo. His companions had already experienced the benefit to be derived from his knowledge of the country's productions, and were beginning to consult him in almost every difficulty that occurred. He appeared capable of accomplishing almost anything.

For all this, they were no little surprised and somewhat incredulous when he declared his intention of climbing the great durion-tree. Murtagh was very much inclined to deny that he could do it.

"The nigger's makin' game of us, captin," he

said. "It would be as much as a squirrel could do to speel up that tall trunk. Why, it's as smooth as the side of a copper-bottomed ship, an' nothin' to lay howlt on. He's jokin'."

"No jokee, Mista Multa. Saloo that tlee climb soon. You help you see."

"Oh, be aisy now! I'll help you all I can, if that'll do any good. How do you mane to set about it?"

To this Saloo made no verbal rejoinder, but laying hold of a small axe, that had been brought away in the boat, he walked off toward a clump of bamboos growing near the spot where they had made their camp.

The first thing he did was to cut down five or six of the largest of these canes, some of them being several inches in diameter, directing Murtagh to drag them off, and deposit them close to the durion-tree.

As soon as he had felled what he deemed a sufficient number, he returned to the spot where the Irishman had deposited them, and commenced chopping them into pieces of about eighteen inches in length. In this the ship-carpenter, by reason of his calling, was able to give him efficient aid; and the ground was soon strewed with disjointed bamboos. Each of the pieces was then split into two, and sharply pointed at one end, so as to resemble a peg designed for being driven into the ground. But it was not into the ground Saloo intended driving them, as will be presently seen.

While Murtagh was engaged in splitting and sharpening the sections of bamboo, the Malay went off once more into the woods, and soon came back again, bearing in his arms what looked like a quantity of rough packing-cord. The freshly-cut ends of it, however, with their greenish color and running sap, told it to be some species of creeping-plant—one of the parasites, or epiphytes, that abound everywhere in the forests of Borneo, as in those of all tropical countries, and render the trade of the ropemaker altogether superfluous.

Throwing down his bundle of creepers, Saloo now took up one of the pointed pegs, and, standing by the trunk of the durion, drove it into the soft sapwood, a little above the height of his own head. The axe, which was a light one, and had a flat hammer-shaped head, served him for a mallet.

As soon as the first peg had been driven to the depth of several inches, he threw aside the axe, and laid hold of the stake with both hands. Then drawing his feet from the ground, so that all his weight came upon the peg, he tried whether it would sustain him without yielding. It did, and he was satisfied.

His next movement was another excursion into the forest, where he found some bamboo stems of a slenderer kind than those already cut, but quite as tall. Having selected three or four of these, he chopped them down, and dragged them up to the durion. Then taking one, he set it upright on its butt-end, parallel to the trunk of the tree, and at such a distance from it as to strike near the outer extremity of the peg already driven home, close to the end of which he had already cut a couple of notches.

Some of the vegetable twine was next prepared by him, and taking a piece of the proper length, he made the upright bamboo fast to the horizontal peg by a knowing knot, such as only a savage or sailor can tie.

Captain Redwood and his ship-carpenter having now obtained an inkling of his design, stood by to render every assistance, while the young people as spectators were very much interested in the proceeding.

As soon as the upright cane was securely lashed to the cross-piece, and also made safe against shifting by having its lower end " stepped" or embedded in the ground, Saloo prepared to ascend, taking with him several of the pegs that had been sharpened. Murtagh " gave him a leg," and he stood upon the first "round" of the ladder.

Then reaching up he drove in a second peg— not quite so far above the first as this was from the ground. With another piece of creeper he made it also fast to the perpendicular pole, and the second round was formed, upon which he had to climb without any helping hand, and with the agility of an ape.

A third step was similarly established; then a fourth and fifth, and so on, till the pegs and cordage carried up with him gave out, when he came back to the ground to provide himself with a second supply. Obtaining this, he once more ascended, and continued to carry aloft his singular " shrouds."

The next thing to be exhausted was the upright piece, which, being only about thirty feet in length, and requiring a surplus to be left, of course came far short of reaching to the lowest limbs of the durion. Another similar stem of bamboo had to be added on by splicing; but for this he did not need to descend, as Murtagh, stretching to his arm's length, handed it up to him, so that he was enabled to lay hold of and draw it up of himself.

Giving the two pieces a good length of double for the splice, he bound them securely together, and then went on with the driving of his pegs, to complete the remaining rounds of the ladder.

In a space of time that did not in all exceed twenty minutes, he had got up to within ten or twelve feet of the lower branches of the durion—to such a height as caused those looking at him from below to feel giddy as they gazed. It was, indeed, a strange and somewhat fearful spectacle—that slight human form, sixty or seventy feet above their heads, at such a vast elevation so diminished in size as to appear like a child or a pigmy, and the more fearful to them who could not convince themselves of the security of the slender stair upon which he was standing. They were half expecting that, at any moment, one of the pegs would give way, and precipitate the poor fellow to the earth, a crushed and shapeless mass!

It was just as when some courageous workman in a manufacturing town—bricklayer or carpenter—ascends to the top of one of its tall factory chimneys, to repair some damage done by firecrack or lightning, and the whole populace of the place rushes out of doors, to look up at the strange spectacle, and admire the daring individual, while trembling in fear for his fate.

So stood the little party under the tall duriontree, regarding the ascent of Saloo.

CHAPTER XV.

SOMETHING SHARP.

THE Malay had ascended, as already said, to within ten or twelve feet from the lower limbs of the tree, and was still engaged driving in his pegs and binding on the upright bamboo to continue his ascent, when all at once he was seen to start and abruptly suspend operations. At the same time an exclamation escaped his lips, in a low tone, but seemingly in accents of alarm.

They all looked up apprehensively, and also started away from the tree; for they expected to see him come tumbling down in their midst. But no; he was still standing firm upon the last made round of the ladder, and in an erect attitude, as if he had no fear of falling. With one hand he held the axe, the other gently grasping the upright bamboo that served him for a support. Instead of looking down to them, to call out or claim their assistance, they saw that his eyes were turned upward and fixed, as if on some object directly over his head. It did not appear to be among the branches of the durion, but as if in the trunk of the tree; and in the interval of silence that succeeded his first quick exclamation, they could hear a hissing sound, such as might proceed from the throat of a goose when some stranger intrudes upon the domain of the farmyard. As it was carried down the smooth stem of the durion, which acted as a conductor, the spectators underneath guessed it was not a goose, but some creature of a less innocent kind.

"A snake, be japers!" was the conjecture that dropped from the ship-carpenter's lips, while the same thought occurred simultaneously to the others; for they could think of no living thing, other than a serpent, capable of sending forth such a sibilant sound as that just heard.

"What is it, Saloo?" hailed Captain Redwood; "are you in any danger?"

"No dangee, cappen; only little bit good luck, that all," was the cheering response that restored their confidence.

"How good luck?" asked the captain, puzzled to think of what fortune could have turned up in their favor so high above their heads.

"You see soon," rejoined the Malay, taking a fresh peg from his girdle and once more resuming his task at stair-making.

While he was engaged in hammering, and between

the resounding strokes, they at the bottom of the tree repeatedly heard the same hissing sound they had taken for the sibilations of a snake, and which they might still have believed to be this, but for a hoarse croaking voice mingling with the sibilation, which reached their ears at intervals, evidently proceeding from the same throat.

Moreover, as they continued to gaze upward, watching Saloo at his work, they caught sight of something in motion on the trunk, and about a foot above his face. It was something of a whitish color and slender shape, pointed like one of the bamboo pegs he was busily driving at. Now they saw it, and now they did not see it; for whatever it was, it was sunk inside the trunk of the durion-tree, alternately protruding and drawing back. It was also clear to them that from this sharp pointed thing, whether beast, bird, or reptile, came the hissing and hoarse croaking that puzzled them.

"What is it?" again asked the captain, now no longer anxious or alarmed, but only curious to know what the strange creature could be.

"Buld, cappen—biggee buld."

"Oh, a bird, that's all; what sort of bird?"

"Honbill; ole hen honbill. She on ha ness inside, hatchee egg; she built up in dat; ole cock he shuttee up with mud."

"Oh, a hornbill!" said the captain, repeating the name of the bird for the information of those around him; and now that they more narrowly scrutinized the spot where the white-pointed beak was still bobbing out and in, they could perceive that there was a patch or space of irregular roundish shape, slightly elevated above the bark, having a plastered appearance, and of the color of dry mud. They had barely time to make this last observation, when Saloo, having got another peg planted so as to enable him to ascend high enough, turned the edge of his axe against the trunk of the durion, and commenced chipping off the mud, that now fell in flakes to the bottom of the tree.

It took him only a very short time to effect a breach into the barricaded nest—one big enough to admit his hand with the fingers at full spread.

His arm was at once thrust in up to the elbow; and as his digits closed fearlessly around the throat of the old hen hornbill, she was drawn forth from her place of imprisonment.

For a time she was seen in Saloo's hands, convulsively writhing and flopping her great wings, like a turkey gobbler with his head suddenly cut off. There was some screaming, hissing, and croaking, but to all these sounds Saloo quickly put an end, by taking a fresh grasp of the throat of the great bird, choking the breath out of it until the wings ceased fluttering; and then he flung its body down at the feet of the spectators.

Saloo did not descend immediately, but once

more thrust his hand into the nest, hoping, no doubt, to find an egg or eggs in it. Instead of these, the contents proved to be a bird—and only one—a chick recently hatched, about the size of a squab pigeon, and fat as a fed ortolan. Unlike the progeny of the megapodes, hatched in the hot sand, the infant hornbill was without the semblance of a feather upon its skin, which was all over of a green, yellowish hue. There was not even so much as a show of down upon it.

For a moment Saloo held it in his hand, hissing as it was in his own tiny way. Then chucking it down after its murdered mother, where it fell not only killed, but "squashed," he prepared to descend in a less hasty manner. He now saw no particular need for their dining on durions, at least on that particular day; and therefore discontinued his task upon the bamboo ladder, which could be completed on the morrow, or whenever the occasion called for it.

CHAPTER XVI.

AN ENEMY IN THE AIR.

THOUGH the old hen hornbill, after her long and seemingly forced period of incubation, might not prove such a tender morsel, they were nevertheless rejoiced at this accession to their now exhausted larder, and the pilot at once set about plucking her, while Murtagh kindled a fresh fire.

While they were thus engaged, Henry, who had greatly admired the ingenuity displayed by Saloo in the construction of his singular ladder, bethought him of ascending it. He was led to this exploit partly out of curiosity to try what such a climb would be like; but more from a desire to examine the odd nest so discovered—for to him, as to most boys of his age, a bird's nest was a peculiarly attractive object. He thought that Saloo had not sufficiently examined the one first plundered, and that there might be another bird or an egg behind. He was not naturalist enough to know—what the ex-pilot's old Sumatran experience had long ago taught him—that the hornbill only lays one egg, and brings forth but a single chick. Whether or no, he was determined to ascend and satisfy himself.

He had no fear of being able to climb the tree-ladder. It did not seem any more difficult than swarming up the shrouds of a ship, and not half so hard as going round the main-top without crawling through the "lubber's hole"—a feat he had often performed on his father's vessel. Therefore, without asking leave, or saying a word to any one, he laid hold of the bamboo pags and started up the tree.

None of the others had taken any notice of him. Captain Redwood was engaged in wiping out his gun, with little Helen attending upon him, while Saloo was playing poulterer, and Murtagh, a little way off in the woods, gathering faggots for the fire. Henry kept on, hand over hand, and foot after foot, till he at length stood upon the topmost round of the unfinished ladder. Being almost as tall as Saloo himself, he easily got his arm into the cavity that contained the nest, and commenced groping all over it. He could find no other bird, nor yet an egg. Only the dried-up ordure of the denizens that had lately occupied the prison cell, along with some bits of the shell out of which the young hornbill had been but recently hatched.

After a moment or two spent in examining the curious cavity, and reflecting on the odd habit of a bird being thus plastered up and kept for weeks in close confinement—all, too, done by its own mate, who surely could not so act from any intention of cruelty—after in vain puzzling himself as to what could be the object of such a singular imprisonment, he determined upon returning to the ground, and seeking the explanation from Saloo.

He had returned upon the topmost step, and was about letting himself down to that next below, when not only were his ears assailed by sharp cries, but he suddenly saw his eyes in danger of being dug out of their sockets by the sharp beak of a bird, whose huge shadowy wings were flapping before his face!

Although somewhat surprised by the onslaught, so sudden and unexpected—and at the same time no little alarmed—there was no mystery about the matter. For he could see at a glance that the bird so assailing him was a hornbill; and a moment's reflection told him it was the cock.

Afar off in the forest—no doubt in search of food —catering for his housekeeper and their new chick, of whose birth he was most probably aware, he could not have heard her cries of distress; else would he have rushed to the rescue, and appeared much sooner upon the scene. But at length he had arrived; and with one glance gathered in the ruin that had occurred during his absence. There was his carefully plastered wall pulled down, the interior of his domicile laid open, his darling ones, no doubt dragged out, throttled and slaughtered, by the young robber still standing but a step from the door.

The enraged parent did not pause to look downward, else he might have seen a still more heartrending spectacle at the bottom of the tree. He did not stay for this; on the instant he went swoop at the head of the destroyer, with a scream that rang far over the forest, and echoed in a thousand reverberations through the branches of the trees.

Fortunately for Henry, he had on his head a thick cloth cap, with its crown cotton-padded. But for this, which served as a helmet, the beak of the bird would have been into his skull, for at the first dab it struck right at his crown.

At the second onslaught, which followed quick after, Henry, being warned, was enabled to ward off the blow, parrying with one hand, while with the other supporting himself on his perch. For all this the danger was not at an end; as the bird, instead of being scared away, or showing any signs of an intention to retreat, only seemed to become more infuriated by the resistance, and continued its swooping and screaming more vigorously and determinedly than ever. The boy was well aware of the peril that impended; and so, too, were those below; who, of course, at the first screech of the hornbill, had looked up and seen what was passing above them.

They would have called upon him to come down, and he would have done so without being summoned, if there had been a chance. But there was none: for he could not descend a single step without using both hands on the ladder; and to do this would leave his face and head without protection. Either left unguarded for a single instant, and the beak of the bird playing about like a pickaxe, would be struck into his skull, or buried deep in the sockets of his eyes. He knew this, and so also they who looked from below. He could do nothing but keep his place, and continue to fight off the furious assailant with his free arm—the hand getting torn at each contact, till the blood could be seen trickling from the tips of his fingers.

It is difficult to say how long this curious contest might have continued, or how it would have terminated, had the combatants been left to themselves. In all probability it would have ended by the boy's having his skull cleft open or his eyes torn out; or, growing feeble, he would have lost his hold upon the ladder and fallen to the foot of the tree—of itself certain death.

It in reality looked as if this would be the

lamentable result, and very quickly. Saloo had sprung to the tree, and was already ascending to the rescue. But for all that he might be too late; or even if successful in reaching the elevated point where Henry struggled against danger, he might still be unable to effect his deliverance. The alarmed father seemed to fear this, as he stood gazing, with agony depicted on his face—agony at the thought of seeing his dear boy exposed to such a fearful peril, and feeling himself so helpless to rescue him.

All at once a thought flashed into his mind, that at least gave him some relief through the necessity of action. His rifle, which fortunately after cleaning he had reloaded, stood resting against the trunk of the tree. He sprang toward and seized hold of it. In another second it was raised to his shoulder; its muzzle pointed almost vertically upward, and circling around to get bearing upon the body of the bird.

It was a dangerous shot to take, like that of Tell with the arrow and the apple. But it seemed yet more dangerous not to venture it; and with this reflection passing through his mind he watched the hornbill through several of its swoopings, and when at length in one of the seit receded to some distance from Henry's face, he took quick sight upon it, and pulled trigger.

A splendid shot—a broken wing—a huge bird

seen fluttering through the air to the earth—then flopping and screaming over the ground, till its cries were stilled and its strugglings terminated by a few blows from a boat-hook held in the hands of the ship-carpenter;—all this was the spectacle of only a few seconds.

CHAPTER XVII.

SITTING BY THE SPIT.

ALOO had by this time climbed to the topmost rounds of the ladder; and was able to assist Henry in descending, which he did without further difficulty or danger.
No great harm had happened to him; he had received only a few scratches and skin-wounds, that would soon yield to careful treatment and the surgical skill which his father possessed, along with certain herbal remedies known to Saloo.

They were soon restored to their former state of equanimity, and thought nothing more of the little incident that had just flurried them, except to congratulate themselves on having so unexpectedly added to their stock of provisions the bodies of two great birds, each of respectable size; to say nothing of the fat featherless chick, which appeared as if it would make a very *bonne bouche* for a gourmand.

As we have said, Saloo did not think any more of ascending the durion-tree, nor they of asking him to do so. Its fruits might have served them for dessert, to come after the game upon which they were now going to dine.

But they were not in condition to care for following the usual fashion of dining, and least of all did they desire a dinner of different courses, so long as they had one sufficiently substantial to satisfy the simple demands of hunger. The two hornbills promised, each of them, a fair *pièce-de-resistance*, while the fat pult was plainly a tit-bit, to be taken either *hors d'œuvres*, or as an *entrée*.

They were not slow in deciding what should be done with the stock so unexpectedly added to their larder. In a trice the cock bird was despoiled of his plumage; the hen having been well-nigh dismantled of hers already. The former was trussed and made ready for the spit, the latter being intended for the pot, on the supposition that boiling might be better for her toughness. Murtagh had taken to finishing the plucking of the hen, while Saloo set about divesting the old cock of his feathers.

The chick needed no plucking, nor even to be singed. Its skin was as free of covering as the shell of the egg lately containing it. It was tender enough to be cooked in any way. It could be broiled over the embers, and would make a nice meal for the two young people, and doubtless greatly benefit their strength.

When the bodies of the old birds were unmasked of their feathery envelopment, it was seen that they were much smaller than supposed; and, moreover, that the hen was by many degrees larger in size and fatter than the cock. It was but natural, and was due to her sex, as well as to her long confinement in a dark cell of but limited dimensions, where she had nothing to do but to rest.

But as the cock bird, after all, was quite as large as a Cochin-China fowl, and, moreover, in good condition, there would be enough of him to supply a full repast, without touching either the hen or chick. So it was determined that both should be reserved till the following morning, when no doubt all hands would be again hungry enough for the toughest of fowls.

This point settled, the old cock was staked upon a bamboo spit, and set over the fire, where he soon began to sputter, sending out a savory odor that was charmingly appetizing.

The hen was at the same time chopped into small pieces, which were thrown into one of the great shells, along with some seasoning herbs Saloo had discovered in the neighboring woods; and as they could now give the stew plenty of time to simmer, it was expected that before next day the toughness would be taken out of the meat, and after all it might prove a palatable dish to people distressed as they had been, and not caring much for mere dainties.

As they had nothing else to do but watch the spit, now and then turn it, and wait till the roast should be done, they fell into conversation, which naturally turned upon hornbills and their habits, Saloo furnishing most of the information concerning these curious birds.

Captain Redwood had not only seen them before, in the course of his voyages among the Malayan Archipelago, but he had read about their habits, and knew that they were found in various parts of the African continent.

They are there called *Korwé* (*Tockus erythrorhynchus*), and Dr. Livingstone gives an interesting account of them.

He says,—" We passed the nest of a korwé, just ready for the female to enter; the orifice was plastered on both sides, but a space left of a heart shape, and exactly the size of the bird's body. The hole in the tree was in every case found to be prolonged some distance above the opening, and thither the korwé always fled to escape being caught."

The first time that Dr. Livingstone himself saw the bird, it was caught by a native, who informed him that when the female hornbill enters her nest, she submits to a positive confinement. The male plasters up the entrance, leaving only a narrow slit by which to feed his mate, and which exactly suits the form of his beak. The female makes a nest of her own feathers, lays her eggs, hatches them, and remains with the young till they are fully fledged. During all this time, which is stated to be two or three months, the male continues to feed her and her young family.

Strange to say, the prisoner generally becomes fat, and is esteemed a very dainty morsel by the natives, while the poor slave of a husband gets so lean that, on the sudden lowering of the temperature, which sometimes happens after a fall of rain, he is benumbed, falls down, and dies.

It is somewhat unusual, as Captain Redwood remarked, for the prisoner to fatten, while the keeper pines!

The toucan of South America also forms her nest in the cavity of a tree, and, like the hornbill, plasters up the aperture with mud.

The hornbill's beak, added Captain Redwood, is slightly curved, sharp-pointed, and about two inches long.

While the body of the rooster was sputtering away in the bright blaze, Saloo entertained the party by telling them what *he* knew about the habits of the hornbills; and this was a good deal, for he had often caught them in the forests of Sumatra. It may be remarked here, that many of the natives of the Malayan Archipelago possess a considerable knowledge of natural history, at least of its practical part. The reason is, that the Dutch who own numerous settlements throughout these islands, have always been great taxidermists and skin-preservers, and to procure specimens for them and obtain the reward, has naturally originated a race of collectors among the native people. Saloo himself had been one of these bird-hunters, in early life, before taking to the sea, which last, as a general thing, is the favorite element and profession of a Malay.

He told them that he knew of two kinds of hornbill in his native island of Sumatra, but that he had seen the skins of several other species in the hands of the taxidermists, brought from various islands, as well as from the mainland of India, Malacca, and Cochin-China. They were all large birds, though some were smaller than the others; mostly black, with white markings about the throat and breast. He said that their nests are always built in the hollow of a tree, in the same way as the one he had robbed, and the entrance to them invariably plastered up with mud in a similar fashion, leaving a hole just big enough to allow the beak of the hen to be passed out, and opened a little for the reception of the food brought to her by her mate. It is the cock that does the "bricking up," Saloo said, bringing the "mortar" from the banks of some neighboring pool or stream, and laying it on with his beak. He begins the task as soon as the hen takes her seat upon her solitary egg. The hen is kept in her prison not only during the full period of incubation, but long after; in fact, until the young chick becomes a full fledgling, and can fly out of itself. During all this time the imprisoned bird is entirely dependent on her mate for every morsel of food required, either by herself or for the sustenance of the nursling, and, of course, has to trust to his fidelity, in which he never fails. The hornbills, however, like the eagles, and many other rapacious birds, though not otherwise of a very amiable disposition, are true to the sacred ties of matrimony. So said Saloo, though not in this exact phraseology.

"But what if the ould cock shud get killed?" suggested Murtagh. "Supposin' any accident was to prevint him from returnin' to the nest? Wud the hen have to stay there an' starve?"

Saloo could not answer this question. It was a theory he had never thought of, or a problem that had not come under his experience. Possibly it might be so; but it was more likely that her imprisonment within the tree cave, being an act agreed to on her part, was more apparent than real, and that she could break through the mud barricade, and set herself free whenever she had a mind to do so.

This was the more probable view of the case, and terminated the discussion on natural history; or rather, it was brought to a close by their perceiving that the bird upon the bamboo stake was done to a turn, and they were by this time too hungry to think of anything else than eating it.

So off it came from the spit, and at it they went with a will, Saloo acting as carver, and distributing the roast joints all around, taking care to give the tenderest bits of breast to the children, and to Helen the liver wing.

They were all very cheerful in commencing their supper, but their strain was changed to sadness even before they had finished it.

CHAPTER XVIII.

SICK AFTER SUPPER.

T was near upon sundown when the roast fowl was taken from the spit, carved, and distributed among them. The fire over which they had cooked it was close to the trunk of the tree under whose shade they intended to pass the night. It was not the one they had chosen after being driven from the durion, but another, with far-spreading branches and green glossy leaves growing thickly upon them, which promised a better protection from the dews of the night. They needed this, as they had not yet thought of erecting any other roof. The only thing in the shape of shelter they had set up was the tarpaulin, spread awning fashion over four uprights, which held it at the four corners; but this was barely sufficient to furnish the two young people with a sleeping-place.

After removing the roast fowl from the spit, they

had not permitted their fire to die out. On the contrary, Murtagh, in whose charge it was, threw on some fresh faggots. They intended keeping it up through the night, not to scare away wild beasts, for, as already said, they had no fear of these; but because the atmosphere toward midnight usually became damp and chilly, and they would need the fire to keep them warm.

It was quite sunset by the time they had finished eating the roast hornbill, and as there is but little twilight under or near the equator, the darkness came down almost instantaneously. By the light of the blazing faggots they picked the bones of the bird, and picked them clean. But they had scarce dropped the drumsticks and other bones out of their fingers, when one and all fell violently sick.

A sensation of vertigo had been growing upon them, which, as soon as the meal was over, became nausea, and shortly after ended in vomiting. It was natural they should feel alarmed. Had only one been ill, they might have ascribed the illness to some other cause; but now, when all five were affected at the same time, and with symptoms exactly similar, they could have no other belief than that it was owing to what they had eaten, and that the flesh of the hornbill had caused their sickness—perhaps poisoned them.

Could this be? Was it possible for the flesh of a bird to be poisonous? Was that of a hornbill so? These questions were quickly asked of one another, but more especially addressed to Saloo. The Malay did not believe it was. He had eaten hornbills before, and more than once; had seen others eat them; but had never known or heard of the dish being followed by symptoms similar to those now affecting and afflicting them.

The bird itself might have eaten something of a poisonous nature, which, although it had not troubled its own stomach, acted as an emetic upon theirs. There was some probability in this conjecture; at all events the sufferers thought so for a time, since there seemed no other way of accounting for the illness which had so suddenly seized upon them.

At first they were not so very greatly alarmed, for they could not realize the idea that they had been absolutely poisoned. A little suffering and it would be all over, when they would take good care not to eat roast hornbill again. No, nor even stewed or broiled; so that now the old hen and her young one were no longer looked upon as so much provision ahead. Both would be thrown away, to form food for the first predatory creature that might chance to light upon them.

As time passed, however, and the sufferers, instead of feeling relieved, only seemed to be growing worse—the vertigo and nausea continuing, while the vomiting was renewed in frequent and violent attacks—they at length became seriously alarmed, believing themselves poisoned to death.

They knew not what to do. They had no medicine to act as an antidote; and if they had been in possession of all the drugs in the pharmacopœia, they would not have known which to make use of. Had it been the bite of a venomous snake or other reptile, the Malay, acquainted with the usual native remedies, might have found some herbaceous balsam in the forest; though in the darkness there would have been a difficulty about this, since it was now midnight, and there was no moon in the sky—no light to look for anything. They could scarcely see one another, and each knew where his neighbors lay only by hearing their moans and other exclamations of distress.

As the hours dragged on wearily, they became still more and more alarmed. They seriously believed that death was approaching. A terrible contemplation it was, after all they had passed through; the perils of shipwreck, famine, thirst; the danger of being drowned; one of them escaping from a hideous reptile; another from the coils of a serpent; a third from having his skull cracked in by a fallen fruit, and afterward split open by the beak of an angry bird. Now, after all these hair-breadth perils and escapes, to be poisoned by eating the flesh of this very bird—to die in such simple and apparently causeless fashion; though it may seem almost ridiculous, it was to them not a whit the less appalling. And appalled they were, as time passed, and they felt themselves growing worse instead of better. They were surely poisoned—surely going to die.

CHAPTER XIX.

AN UNEASY NIGHT

ALONG with the agonizing pain—for the sensations they experienced were exceedingly painful—there was confusion in their thoughts, and wandering in their speech. The feeling was somewhat similar to that of sea-sickness in its worst form; and they felt that reckless indifference to death so characteristic of the sufferer from this very common, but not the less painful, complaint. Had the sea, seething and surging against the beach so near them, broken beyond its boundaries, and swept over the spot where they lay, not one of them, in all probability, would have stirred hand or foot to remove themselves out of its reach. Drowning—death in any form—would at that moment have seemed preferable to the tortures they were enduring.

They did not lie still. At times one or another would get up and stray from under the tree. But the nausea continued, accompanied by the horrid retching; their heads swam, their steps tottered, and staggering back they would fling themselves down despairingly, hoping, almost praying, for death to put an end to their agonies. It was likely soon to do so.

During all, Captain Redwood showed that he was thinking less of himself than his children. Willingly would he have lain down and died, could that have secured their surviving him. But it was a fate that threatened all alike. On this account he was wishing that either he or one of his comrades, Murtagh or Saloo, might outlive the young people long enough to give them the rites of sepulture. He could not bear the thought that the bodies of his two beautiful children were to be left above ground, on the desolate shore, their flesh to be torn from them by the teeth of ravenous beasts or the beaks of predatory birds—their bones to whiten and moulder under the sun and storms of the tropics.

Despite the pain he was himself enduring, he secretly communicated his wishes to Murtagh and the Malay, imploring them to obey what might be almost deemed a dying request.

Parting speeches were from time to time exchanged in the muttered tones of despair. Prayers were said aloud, unitedly, and by all of them silently in their own hearts.

After this, Captain Redwood lay resignedly, his children, one on each side of him, nestling within his arms, their heads pillowed upon his breast close together. They also held one another by the hand, joined in affectionate embrace across the breast of their father. Not many words were spoken between them; only, now and then, some low murmurs, which betokened the terrible pain they felt, and the fortitude both showed in enduring it.

Now and then, too, their father spoke to them. At first he had essayed to cheer them with words of encouragement; but as time passed, these seemed to sound hollow in their ears as well as his own, and he changed them to speeches enjoining resignation, and words that told of the "Better Land." He reminded them that their mother was there, and they should all soon join her. They would go to her together; and how happy this would be after their toils and sufferings; after so many perils and fatigues, it would be but pleasure to find rest in heaven.

In this way he tried to win their thoughts from dwelling on the terrors of death, every moment growing darker and seeming nearer.

The fire burned down, smouldered, and went out. No one had thought of replenishing it with fuel. Though there were faggots enough collected not far off, the toil of bringing them forward seemed too much for their wasted strength and deadened energies. Fire could be of no service to them now. It had done them no good while ablaze; and since it had gone out, they cared not to renew it. If they were to die, their last moments could scarcely be more bitter in darkness than in light.

Still Captain Redwood wished for light. He wished for it, so that he might once more look upon the faces of his two sweet suffering pets, before the pallor of death should overspread them. He would perhaps have made an effort to rekindle the fire, or requested one of the others to do it; but just then, on turning his eyes to the east, he saw a grayish streak glimmering above the line of the sea horizon. He knew it was the herald of coming day; and he knew, moreover, that, in the latitude they were in, the day itself would not linger long behind.

"Thank God!" was the exclamation that came from his lips, low muttered, but in fervent emphasis. "Thank God, I shall see them once more! Better their lives should not go out in the darkness."

As he spoke the words, and as if to gratify him, the streak on the eastern sky seemed rapidly to grow broader and brighter, its color of pale gray changing to golden yellow; and soon after the upper limb of the glorious tropical sun showed itself over the smooth surface of the Celebes Sea.

As his cheering rays touched the trees of the forest, their eyes were first turned upon one another, and then in different directions. Those of Captain Redwood rested upon the faces of his children, now truly overspread with the wan pallor of what seemed to be rapidly approaching death.

Murtagh gazed wistfully out upon the ocean, as if wishing himself once more upon it, and no doubt thinking of that green isle far away beyond it; while Saloo's glance was turned upward—not toward the heavens, but as if he was contemplating some object among the leaves of the tree overhead.

All at once the expression upon his countenance took a change—remarkable as it was sudden. From the look of sullen despair, which but the moment before might have been seen gleaming out of the sunken orbits of his eyes, his glance seemed to change to one of joy, almost with the quickness of the lightning's flash.

Simultaneous with the change, he sprang up from his reclining position, uttering as he did so an exclamation in the Malayan tongue, which his companions guessed to be some formula of address to the Deity, from its ending with the word "Allah."

"De gleat God be thank!" he continued, returning to his "pigeon English," so that the others might understand. "We all be save. Buld no poison. We no die yet. Come away, cappen," he continued, bending down, and seizing the children by the hands. Then raising both on their feet, he quickly added, "Come all away. Unda de tlee death. Out yonda we findee life. Come away—way."

Without waiting for the consent either of them or their father, he led—indeed, almost dragged—

Helen and Henry from under the shadow of the tree and out toward the open sea-beach.

Though Captain Redwood did not clearly comprehend the object of Saloo's sudden action, nor Murtagh comprehend it at all, both rose to their feet and followed with tottering steps.

Not until they had got out upon the open ground, and sat down upon the sand, with the fresh sea-breeze fanning their fevered brows, did Saloo give an explanation of his apparently eccentric behavior.

He did so by pointing to the tree under which they had passed the night, and pronouncing only the one word—" Upas."

CHAPTER XX.

THE DEADLY UPAS.

PAS! A word sufficient to explain all that had passed. Both Captain Redwood and his ship-carpenter understood its signification; for what man is there who has ever sailed through the islands of the India Archipelago without having heard of the upas? Indeed, who in any part of the world has not either heard or read of this poisonous tree, supposed to carry death to every living thing for a wide distance around it, not even sparing shrubs or plants—things of its own kind—but inflicting blight and destruction wherever its envenomed breath may be wafted on the breeze?

Captain Redwood was a man of too much intelligence, and too well-informed, to have belief in this fabulous tale of the olden time. Still he knew there was enough truth in it to account for all that had occurred—for the vertigo and vomiting, the horrible nausea and utter prostration of strength that had come upon them unconsciously. They had made their camp under one of these baneful trees—the true upas (*antiaris toxicaria*); they had kindled a fire beneath it, building it close to the trunk—in fact, against it; the smoke had ascended among its leaves; the heat had caused a sudden exudation of the sap; and the envenomed vapor floating about upon the air had freely found its way both into their mouths and nostrils. For hours had this empoisoned atmosphere been their only breath, nearly depriving them of that upon which their lives depended.

If still suffering severely from the effects of having inhaled the noxious vapor, they were now no longer wretched. Their spirits were even restored to a degree of cheerfulness, as is always the case with those who have just escaped from some calamity or danger. They now knew that in due time they would recover their health and strength. The glorious tropical sun that had arisen was shining benignantly in their faces, and brightening everything around, while the breeze, blowing fresh upon them from a serene sapphire-colored sea, cooled their fevered blood. They felt already reviving. The sensations they experienced were those of one who, late suffering from sea-sickness, pent up in the state-room of a storm-tossed ship, with all its vile odors around him, has been suddenly transferred to *terra firma*, and laid upon some solid bank, grassy or moss-grown, with tall trees waving above, and the perfume of flowers floating upon the balmy air.

For a long while they sat upon the sands in this pleasant dreamy state, gazing upon the white surf that curled over the coral reefs, gazing upon the blue water beyond, following the flight of large white-winged birds that now and then went plunging down into the sea, to rise up with a fish glistening in their beaks, half unconscious of the scene under their eyes and the strife continuing before them, but conscious, contented, and even joyous at knowing they still lived, and that the time had not yet come for them to die.

They no longer blamed the hornbill for what had happened. The cause was in their own carelessness or imprudence; for Captain Redwood knew the upas tree, and was well aware of its dangerous properties to those venturing into too close proximity. He had seen it in other islands; for it grows not only in Java, with which its name is more familiarly identified, but in Bali, Celebes, and Borneo. He had seen it elsewhere, and heard it called by different names, according to the different localities, as *tayim, hippo, upo, antijar*, and *upas;* all signifying the same thing—the "tree of poison."

Had he been more careful about the selection of their camping-place, and looked upon its smooth reddish or tan-colored bark and closely-set leaves of glossy green, he would have recognized and shunned it. He did not do so; for who at such a time could have been thinking of such a catastrophe? Under a tree whose shade seemed so inviting, who would have suspected that danger was lurking, much less that death dwelt among its leaves and branches?

The first had actually arisen, and the last had been very near. But it was now far away, or at least no longer to be dreaded from the poison of the upas. The sickness caused by it would continue for awhile, and it might be some time before their strength or energies would be fully restored. But of dying there was no danger, as the poison of the upas does not kill, when only inhaled as a vapor; unless the inhalation be a long time continued. Its sap taken internally, by the chewing of its leaves, bark, or root, is certain death, and speedy death. It is one of the ingredients used by the Bornean Dyaks for tipping their poisoned spears, and the arrows of their *sumpitans* or blow-guns. They use it in combination with the *bina*, another deadly poison, extracted from the juice of a parasitical plant found everywhere through the forests of Borneo.

It is singular that the upas-tree should belong to the same natural order, the Artocarpaceæ, as the bread-fruit; the tree of death thus being connected with the tree of life. In some of the Indian islands it is called *Popon-upas;* in Java it is known as the *Antijar.*

Its leaves are shaped like spear-heads: the fruit is a kind of drupe, clothed in fleshy scales.

The juice, when prepared as a poison, is sometimes mixed with black pepper, and the juice of galanga-root, and of ginger. It is as thick as molasses, and will keep for a long time if sheltered from the action of the air.

The upas does not grow as a gregarious tree, and is nowhere found in numbers. Like the precious treasures of nature—gold, diamonds, and pearls—her poisons, too, happily for man, are sparsely distributed. Even in the climate and soil congenial to it, the *antiaris toxicaria* is rare; but wherever discovered is sure to be frequently visited, if in a district where there are hunters or warriors wishing to empoison and make more deadly their shafts. A upas-tree in a well-known neighborhood is usually disfigured by seams and scars, where incisions have been made to extract its envenomed juice.

That there were no such marks upon the one where they had made their camp, was evidence that the neighborhood was uninhabited. So said Saloo, and the others were but too glad to accept his interpretation of the sign.

CHAPTER XXI.

STARTING FOR THE INTERIOR.

RECLINING on the soft silvery sand, inhaling the fresh morning breeze blowing in from the Celebes Sea, every breath of it seeming to infuse fresh blood into their veins and renewed vigor into their limbs, the castaways felt their health and strength fast returning. Saloo's prognosis was rapidly proving itself correct. He had said they would soon recover, and they now acknowledged the truth of his prediction.

Their cheerfulness came back along with their returning strength, and with this also their appetites. Their dinner-supper of roast hornbill had done them little good; but although for a time scared by such diet, and determined to eschew it when better could be had, they were now only too glad to resort to it, and it was agreed upon that the old hen, stewed as intended, should supply the material of their breakfast.

A fresh fire was kindled far away from the dangerous upas; the huge shell, with its contents, was hastily snatched from the deadly shade, and supported by four large pebbles to serve as feet for the queer stew-pan, it was placed over the burning embers, and soon commenced to steam and squeak, spreading around an odorous incense, far pleasanter to the olfactories of the hungry party than either the fresh saline breeze, or the perfume of tropical flowers now and then wafted to them from the recesses of the forest.

While waiting for the flesh of the old hen to get properly and tenderly stewed, they could not resist the temptation of making an assault upon the chick; and it, too, was hurriedly rescued from the tainted larder beneath the upas-tree, spitted upon a bamboo sapling, and broiled like a squab-pigeon over the incandescent brands.

It gave them only a small morsel each, serving as a sort of prelude to the more substantial breakfast soon to follow, and for which they could now wait with greater composure.

In due time Saloo, who was wonderfully skilled in the tactics of the forest *cuisine*, pronounced the stew sufficiently done; when the stew-pan was lifted from the fire, and set in the soft sand for its contents to cool.

Soon gathering around it, each was helped to a share: one to a wing with liver or gizzard, another to a thigh-joint with a bit of the breast, a third to the stripped breast-bone, or the back one, with its thin covering of flesh, a fourth to a variety of stray giblets.

There was still a savory sauce remaining in the pan, due to the herb condiments which Saloo had collected. This was served out in some tin pannikins, which the castaway crew had found time to fling into the boat before parting from the sinking ship. It gave them a soup, which, if they could only have had biscuits or bread with it, would have been quite as good as coffee for their breakfast.

As soon as this was eaten, they took steps to change their place of encampment. Twice unfortunate in the selection of a site, they were now more particular, and carefully scrutinized the next tree under whose shadow they intended to take up their abode. A spreading fig not far off invited them to repose beneath its umbrageous foliage; and removing their camp paraphernalia from the poison-breathing upas, they once more erected the tarpaulin, and recommenced housekeeping under the protecting shelter of a tree celebrated in the Hindu mythology as the "sacred banyan."

"It was a goodly sight to see
That venerable tree;
For o'er the lawn, irregularly spread,
Fifty straight columns propt its lofty head,
And many a long depending shoot,
Seeking to strike its root,

> Straight like a plummet grew toward the ground.
> Some on the lower boughs which crost their way,
> Fixing their bearded fibres, round and round,
> With many a ring and wild contortion wound;
> Some to the passing wind at times, with sway
>   Of gentle motion swung;
> Others of younger growth, unmoved, were hung
> Like stone-drops from a cavern's fretted height."

The banyan often measures thirty feet in girth; the one selected by Captain Redwood was probably not less than twenty-five feet. Its peculiarity is that it throws out roots from all its branches, so that as fast as each branch, in growing downward, touches the ground, it takes root, and in due time serves as a substantial prop to the horizontal bough, which, without some such support, would give way beneath its own weight.

They intended it for only a temporary dwelling-place, until their strength should be sufficiently established to enable them to start on their contemplated overland journey, with a prospect of being able to continue it to its end.

It seemed, at length, as if fortune, hitherto so adverse, had turned a smiling face toward them; and they were not much longer to be detained upon that wild and dangerous shore. For the same day on which they removed from the upas to the fig-tree, the latter furnished them with an article of food in sufficient quantity to stock their larder for nearly a week, and of a quality superior in strengthening powers to either roast or stewed hornbill, and quite equal to the eggs of the mound-making birds.

It was not the fruit of the fig that had done this; but an animal they had discovered crawling along one of its branches. It was a reptile of that most hideous and horrid shape, the *saurian ;* and only the hungriest man could ever have looked upon, with thoughts of eating it. But Saloo felt no repugnance of this kind; he knew that the huge lizard creeping along the limb of the banyan-tree, over five feet long, and nearly as thick as the body of a man, would afford flesh not only eatable, but such as would have been craved for by Apicius, had the Roman epicure ever journeyed through the islands of the Malayan Archipelago, and found an opportunity of making trial of it.

What they saw slowly traversing the branch above them was one of those huge lizards of the genus *Hydrosaurus*, of which there are several species in Indian climes—like the *iguanas* of America—harmless creatures, despite their horrid appearance, and often furnishing to the hunter or forester a meal of chops and steaks both tender and delicious.

With this knowledge of what it would afford them, Saloo had no difficulty in persuading Captain Redwood to send a bullet through the skull of the *hydrosaurus*, and it soon lay lifeless upon the ground.

The lizard was nigh six feet from snout to tail; and Saloo, assisted by Murtagh, soon slipped a piece of his vegetable rope around its jaws, and slung it up to a horizontal branch for the purpose of skinning it. Thus suspended, with limbs and arms sticking out, it bore a very disagreeable resemblance to a human being just hanged. Saloo did not care anything about this, but at once commenced peeling off its skin; and then he cut the body into quarters, and subdivided them into "collops," which were soon sputtering in the blaze of a bright fire. As the Malay had promised, these proved tender, tasting like young pork steaks, with a slight flavor of chicken, and just a *soupçon* of frog. Delicate as they were, however, after three days' dieting upon them all felt stronger—almost strong enough indeed to commence their grand journey.

Just then another, and still more strengthening kind of food was added to their larder. It was obtained by a mere accident, in the form of a huge wild boar of the Bornean species, which, scouring the forest in search of fruits or roots, had strayed close to their camp under the fig-tree. He came too close for his own safety; a bullet from Captain Redwood's rifle having put an abrupt stop to his "rootings."

Butchered in proper scientific fashion, he not only afforded them food for the time in the shape of pork chops, roast ribs, and the like; but gave them a couple of hams, which, half-cooked and cured by smoking, could be carried as a sure supply upon the journey.

And so provisioned, they at length determined on commencing it, taking with them such articles of the wreck-salvage as could be conveniently transferred, and might prove beneficial. Bidding adieu to the pinnace, the dear old craft which had so safely carried them through the dangers of the deep, they embarked on a voyage of a different kind, in the courses of which they were far less skilled, and of whose tracks and perils they were even more apprehensive. But they had no other alternative. To remain on the eastern coast of Borneo would be to stay there forever. They could not entertain the slightest hope of any ship appearing off shore to rescue them. A vessel so showing itself would be, in all probability, a präu filled with bloodthirsty pirates, who would either kill or make captives of them, and afterward sell them into slavery: and a slavery from which no civilized power could redeem them, as no civilized men might ever see them in their chains.

It was from knowing this terrible truth that Captain Redwood had resolved upon crossing the great island overland at that part where he supposed it to be narrowest,—the neck lying between its eastern coast and the old Malayan town of

Bruñi on the west, adjacent to the islet of Labuan, where he knew an English settlement was situated.

In pursuance of this determination, he struck camp, and moved forward into a forest of unknown paths and mysterious perils.

CHAPTER XXII.

ACROSS COUNTRY.

IN undertaking the journey across Borneo, Captain Redwood knew there would be many difficulties to encounter, as well as dangers. There was first the great distance, which could not be much less than two hundred and fifty miles, even if they should succeed in making it in a straight line—as the crow flies. But, no doubt, obstructions would present themselves along the route to cause many a detour. Still this was an obstacle which time would overcome. At the rate of ten miles a day, it would be conquered in a month; and if two months should have to be spent, it would not be a very formidable hardship, considering that it was a journey overtaken to carry them through a savage wilderness, and restore them to civilization—nay, almost to life.

That it was to be made on foot did not dismay them. They had quite recovered from the effects of their sea-suffering, as also from the poisonous breath of the upas, and felt strong enough to undertake any great feat of pedestrianism. And, as they were under no limits as to time, they could adopt such a rate of speed as the nature of the paths would permit. On this score there was neither apprehension nor uneasiness; there might have been about provisions, as the cured hams of the wild boar could not possibly last longer than a week; and what were they to eat after these were consumed?

Saloo set their minds at rest on this matter, by telling them that the interior forests of Borneo—which he did not know—if they at all resembled those of Sumatra—which he did know—would be found full of fruit-bearing trees; and, besides, numerous chances would arise for killing or capturing birds and other small game, even if a deer or a second wild boar did not present himself. In order to be prepared for any such that might come in his way, as well as to save their ammunition, of which they had but a limited supply, Saloo had spent the last few days of their sojourn upon the coast in the manufacture of a weapon well suited for such a purpose, even better than musket or rifle. It was the "Sumpitan," or blow-gun. This the Malay had made, along with a complete set of "sumpits," or arrows, and a quiver to contain them. The sumpitan itself—eight feet in length—he fashioned from a straight sapling of the beautiful *casuarina* tree, which grows throughout the islands of the Malayan Archipelago; while the little arrows, only eight inches long, he obtained from the medium of the leaflets of the *nibong* palms, many of which were found near the spot where they had encamped. The pith of the same palm served him for the swell of the arrow, which, being compressible like cork, fills up the tube of the sumpitan, and renders the shaft subject to propulsion from the quick puff of breath which the blow-gun marksman, from long practice, knows how to give it.

Saloo had been one of the best sumpitan shooters in all Sumatra, and could send an arrow with true aim a distance of a hundred and fifty yards. But to make its effect deadly at this distance, something more than the mere pricking of the tiny "sumpit" was needed. This something was a strong vegetable poison which he also knew how to prepare; and the upas-tree, that had so nearly proved fatal to all of them, was now called into requisition to effect a friendly service. Drawing upon its sap, and mixing it with that of another poisonous plant —the *bina*—Saloo gave the points of his sumpits a coating of the combined juices, so that they would carry death into the veins of any animal having the ill-fortune to be pierced by them.

Thus armed and equipped, he had little fear on the score of a scarcity of provisions during the journey. On the contrary, he declared himself confident of being able to keep the commissariat up to a point of supply sufficient for the whole party.

It may be thought strange that they did not speculate on the chances of arriving at some town or settlement of the natives. Indeed they did so, but only with the thought of avoiding them; for the minds of all—the Malay not excepted—were filled with apprehensions respecting the Dyak and other savage tribes, which report places in the interior of Borneo, and to whom long accredited, though perhaps only imaginative, stories have given a character alike terrible and mysterious. They could think of them only as savages—wild men of the woods—some of them covered with hair, and whose chief delight and glory are the cutting off men's heads, and not unfrequently feasting on men's flesh! No wonder that, with these facts, or fancies, acting upon their imagination, our travellers set forth upon their journey determined to give a wide berth to everything that bore the shape of a human being. It was a strange commentary on man's superiority to the lower animals, and not very creditable to the former, that he himself was the thing they most feared to meet with in the wooded wilderness. And yet, humiliating as the reflection may appear, it depressed the minds of the castaways, as, looking their last upon the bright blue sea, they turned their faces toward the interior of the forest-covered land of Borneo.

For the first day they pursued a course leading along the bank of the stream at whose mouth they had been sojourning ever since their arrival on the island. They had more than one reason for keeping to the stream. It seemed to flow in a due easterly direction, and therefore to ascend it would lead them due west—the way they wanted to go. Besides, there was a path along its banks, not made by man, but evidently by large animals; whose tracks, seen here and there in soft places, showed them to be tapirs, wild-boars, and the larger but more rare rhinoceros.

They saw none of these animals during their day's journey, though many of the traces were fresh. Generally nocturnal in their habits, the huge pachydermatous creatures that had made them were, during daylight, probably lying asleep in their lairs, amid the thick underwood of the adjacent jungles.

The travellers might have brought the pinnace up the river—so far it was deep enough to be navigated by a row-boat; and they had at first thought of doing so. But for several reasons they had changed their minds, and abandoned their boat. It was too heavy to be easily propelled by oars, especially against the current of a stream which in many places was very rapid. Besides, if there should be a settlement of savages on the bank, to approach in a boat would just be the way to expose themselves to being seen, without first seeing.

But to Captain Redwood the chief objection was, that a mountain-range rose only a short distance off, and the stream appeared to issue from its steep sloping side; in which case it would soon assume the character of a headlong torrent, utterly unfit for navigation. Even had water travel been easier, it could not have been long continued— perhaps not beyond a single day; and it was not deemed worth while to bring the pinnace with them. So thought the captain, and the others agreeing, the boat was left where they had long since concealed her—under the banyan-tree.

The captain's conjectures proved correct. The evening of the first day's march brought them to the base of the mountain-ridge, down whose rocky flank the stream poured with the strength and velocity of a torrent. No boat could have further ascended it.

As the path leading along its edge, and hitherto comparatively level and smooth, now changed to a difficult ascent up a rough rock-strewn ravine, they encamped at the mountain-foot for the first night of their journey.

Next day was spent in ascending the mountain; following the ravine up to its head, where were found the sources of the stream. Staying only for a short noon-tide rest, they kept upward, and reached the highest point of the ridge just as the sun was again sinking into the depths of the forest before them.

At their camping-place on the second night no water was near; and they might have suffered from the want of it, had they not taken the precaution to provide against such a deficiency. Their experience as castaways, especially the memory of their sufferings from thirst, had rendered them wary of being again subjected to so terrible a torture. Each of the three men carried a "canteen" strung to his waist—the joint of a large bamboo that held at least half a gallon; while the boy and girl also had their cane canteens, proportioned to their size and strength. All had been filled with cool clear water before leaving the last source of the stream, a supply sufficient to serve during their transit of the dry mountain-ridge.

The remainder of that night was spent upon its summit; but as this proved of considerable breadth, and was covered with a thick growth of jungle-trees, it was near sunset the next day before they arrived at the edge of its eastern declivity, and obtained a view of the country beyond.

The sun was descending behind the crest of another mountain-ridge, apparently parallel with that upon which they were, and not less than twenty miles distant from it. Between the two extended a valley, or rather a level plain, thickly covered with forest, except where a sheet of water gleamed in the setting sun like a disk of liquid gold.

Nor was the plain all level. Here and there, above the wooded surface, rose isolated hills, of rounded mound-like shape, also clothed with timber, but with trees whose foliage, of lighter sheen, showed them to be of species different from those on the plain below.

Through a break among the branches of those now shadowing them on the mountain brow, the travellers for some time contemplated the country before them, and across which, upon the morrow, they would have to make their way.

At this moment Saloo muttered some words, which, coupled with the expression upon his countenance as he gave utterance to them, alarmed his companions. The words were,—

"It lookee like countly of *mias lombi*. Cappen Ledwad, if dat wild debbel lib in dem wood below, bettel we go all lound. We tly closs it, may be we get eat up. Singapo tiga not so dang'lous as *mias* —he not common kind, but gleat *mias lombi*— what Poltugee people callee '*led golilla.*'"

"The *red gorilla!*" ejaculated Captain Redwood. "Is it the *ourang-outang* you mean?"

"Same ting, Sahib cappen. Some call him *oolang-ootang*, some say *led golilla*. One kind belly big—belly bad—he call *mias lombi*. He cally away women, childen; take 'em up into top ob de highest tallee tlee. Nobody know what he do then. Eat 'em up may be. What fol else he want 'em? Ah! Cappen Ledwad, we dlead de oolang-Dyak. He no half dang'lous like oolang-ootang led golilla."

Notwithstanding the *patois* of his speech, what Saloo said was well enough understood by his companions, for in the *led golilla* or *oolang-ootang* of his peculiar pronunciation, they recognized the long known and world-renowned ape of Borneo, which, although safe enough when seen inside the cage of the showman, is a creature to be dreaded— at least the species spoken of—when encountered in its native haunts, the forests of Sumatra and Borneo.

CHAPTER XXIII.

TOUGH TRAVELLING.

EXT morning they did not start so early, because the great plain before them was shrouded under a fog, and they waited for it to pass off.

It was not dispelled until the sun had risen in the heavens behind them, for their backs were still to the east, their route lying due westward.

During the night, and again in the morning, they had discussed the question of striking straight across the plain, or making a circuitous march around it. When the fog at length lifted, this point was definitely settled by what they saw before and on each side of them, that the great valley plain extended both to right and left beyond the limits of their vision. To go round it might add scores of miles and many days to their journey. They could not think of taking such a circuitous route, even with the fear of the wild men before them; a danger Captain Redwood believed to be greatly exaggerated by the Malay, who in such matters was of somewhat imaginative turn. Throwing aside all thought of such an encounter, they struck down the mountain slope, determined on crossing the plain.

It was sunset when they arrived at the mountain-foot, and another night was passed there.

On the following morning they commenced the passage of the plain; which introduced them to a very different and much more difficult kind of travelling than any they had experienced since leaving the sea-coast. Some parts of their journey, both in the ascent and descent, had been toilsome enough; but the slopes, as well as the summits, were comparatively clear of underwood. On the low level it was quite another affair. The huge forest trees were loaded with parasitical creepers, which, stretching from trunk to trunk in all directions, formed here and there an impenetrable net or trellis-work. In such places the kris of Saloo, and the ship's axe carried by Murtagh, were called into requisition, and much time was expended in cutting a way through the tangled growth.

Another kind of obstacle was also occasionally met with, in the brakes of bamboo, where these gigantic canes, four or five inches in diameter, and rising to a height of over fifty feet, grew so close together that even a snake would have found difficulty in working its way through them. Fortunately, their stems being hollow, they are easily brought down, and a single stroke from the axe, or even Saloo's sharp kris, given slantingly, would send one of them crashing over, its leafy top bearing along with it the long ribbon-like leaves of many others.

One of these cane brakes proved to be upward of a mile in width, and its passage delayed them at least three hours. They might have attempted to get round it, but they did not know how far it extended. Possibly ten or twenty miles—for the bamboo thickets often run in belts, their growth being due to the presence of some narrow water track, or the course of a stream. In the Indian Archipelago are several species of these tall canes, usually known by the general name of *bamboo*, though differing from each other in size and other respects. They furnish to the inhabitants of these islands the material for almost every article required for their domestic economy—as the various species of palms do to the natives of South America— more especially the denizens of the great Amazon valley. Not only are their houses constructed of bamboo, but the greater portion of their präus; while utensils of many kinds, cups, bottles, and water-casks of the best make, are obtained from its huge joints, cheaply and conveniently. A bare catalogue of bamboo tools and utensils would certainly occupy several pages.

Notwithstanding its valuable properties, our

travellers hated the sight of it; and more than once the Irishman, as he placed his axe upon the silicious culms, was heard to speak disrespectfully about it, "weeshin' that there wasn't a stalk of the cane in all Burnayo."

But another kind of obstruction vexed Murtagh even more than the brakes of bamboo. This was the webs of huge spiders—ugly tarantula-looking animals—whose nets in places, extending from tree to tree, traversed the forest in every direction, resembling the seines of a fishing-village hung out to dry, or miles of musquito-curtain depending from the horizontal branches. Through this strange festoonery they had to make their way, often for hundreds of yards; the soft silky substance clutching disagreeably around their throats and clinging to their clothes till each looked as though clad in an integument of ragged cotton, or the long loose wool of a merino sheep yet unwoven into cloth. And as they forced their way through it—at times requiring strength to extricate them from its tough retentive hold—they could see the hideous forms of the huge spiders who had spun and woven these strangely patterned webs scuttling off, and from their dark retreats in the crevices of the trees looking defiant and angry at the intruders upon their domain—perhaps never before trodden by man.

Yet another kind of obstruction our travellers had to encounter on their way across the great plain. There were tracts of moist ground, sometimes covered with tall forest-trees, at others opening out into a sedgy morass, with perhaps a small lake or water-patch in the centre. The first required them to make way through mud, or thick stagnant water covered with scum, often reaching above their knees. These places were especially disagreeable to cross: for under the gloomy shadow of the trees they would now and then catch a glimpse of huge newt-like lizards of the genus *hydrosaurus* —almost as large as crocodiles—slowly floundering out of the way, as if reluctant to leave, and half-determined to dispute the passage.

Moreover, while thus occupied, they lived in the obscurity of an eternal twilight, and could travel only by guess-work. They had no guide save the sun, which in these shadows is never visible. Through the thick foliage overhead its disk could not be seen; nor aught that would enable them to determine its position in the sky, and along with it their direction upon the earth. It was, therefore, not only a relief to their feelings, but a positive necessity for their continuance in the right direction, that now and then a stretch of open swamp obstructed their track. True, it caused them to make a detour, and so wasted their time; but then it afforded them a glimpse of the sun's orb, and enabled them to pursue their journey in the right course.

During the midday hours they were deprived of even this guidance; for the meridian sun gives no clue to the points of the compass. They did not much feel the disadvantage; as at noon-tide the hot tropical atmosphere had become almost insupportable, and the heat, added to their fatigue from incessant toiling through thicket and swamp, made it necessary for them to take several hours of rest.

They resumed their journey in the evening, as the sun, declining toward the western horizon, pointed out to them the way they were to go. They aimed to reach the sheet of water seen by them from the brow of the mountain. They wished to strike it at its southern end, as this was right in the direction westward. It appeared to lie about midway between the two mountain-ranges; and, in such a case, would be a proper halting-place on their journey across the plain.

On starting from the higher ground, they expected to reach it in a few hours or at the latest by sunset of that same day. But it was twilight of the third day, when, with exhausted strength and wearied limbs, their clothing torn and mud-stained, they stood upon its nearest shore! They did not stand there long, but dropping down upon the earth, forgetful of everything—even the necessity of keeping watch—they surrendered themselves over to sleep.

CHAPTER XXIV.

A RED SATYR.

HEY slept until a late hour of the morning; when, rousing themselves with difficulty, they kindled a fire and cooked a breakfast of the boar's ham cured by them before leaving the coast. It was the second, and of course the last, already becoming rapidly reduced to a "knuckle;" for their journey was now entering upon the second week.

They bethought them of making a halt on the bank of the lake; partly to recruit their strength after the long-continued fatigue, and partly, if possible, to replenish their larder.

Saloo got ready his blow-gun and poisoned arrows; Captain Redwood looked to his rifle; while the ship-carpenter, whose specialty was fishing, and who for this purpose had brought his hooks and lines along with him, determined on trying what species of the finny tribe frequented the inland lake, in hopes they might prove less shy at biting than their brethren of the sea-coast stream.

Again the three men started off, Murtagh traversing in solitude the edge of the lake, while Captain Redwood, with his rifle—accompanied by Saloo, carrying his sumpitan and quiver of poisoned arrows—struck direct into the woods.

Henry and Helen remained where they had passed the night, under the shadow of a spreading tree; which, although of a species unknown to the travellers, had been cautiously scrutinized by them, and seemed to be neither a durion nor a upas. They were cautioned not to stir a step from the spot till the others should return.

Though in other respects a good, obedient boy, Henry Redwood was not abundantly gifted with prudence. He was a native-born New Yorker, and as such, of course, precocious, courageous, daring, even to a fault—in short, having the heart of a man beating within the breast of a boy. So inspired, when a huge bird, standing even taller than himself on its great stilt-like legs—it was the adjutant stork of India (*ciconia argalia*)—dropped down upon the point of a little peninsula which projected into the lake, he could not resist the temptation of getting a shot at it.

Grasping the great ship's musket—part of the paraphernalia they had brought along with them, and which was almost as much as he could stagger under—he started to stalk the great crane, leaving little Helen under the tree.

Some reeds growing along the edge of the lake offered a chance by which the game might be approached, and under cover of them he had crept almost within shot of it, when a cry fell upon his ear, thrilling him with a sudden dread.

It was the voice of his sister Helen, uttered in tones of alarm!

Turning suddenly, he wondered not that her cries were continued in the wildest terror, mingled with convulsive ejaculations. A man had drawn near her, and oh! such a man! Never in all his experience, nor in his darkest and most distorted dreams, had he seen, or dreamt of, a human being so hideous as that he now saw, half-standing, half-crouching, only a short distance from his sister's resting-place.

It was a man who, if he had only been in an erect attitude, would have stood at least eight feet in height, and this would have been in an underproportion to the size of his head, the massive breadth of his body across the breast and shoulders, and the length of his arms. But it was not his gigantic size which made him so terrible, or which electrified the heart of the boy, at a safe distance, as it had done that of the girl, nearer and in more danger. It was the *tout ensemble* of this strange creature in human shape—a man apparently cov ered all over with red hair, thick and shaggy, as upon the skin of a wolf or bear; bright red over the body and limbs, and blacker upon the face, where it was thinnest—a creature, in short, such as neither boy nor girl had ever before seen, and such as was long believed to exist only in the imagination of the ancients, under the appellation of "satyr."

CHAPTER XXV.

SILENCE RESTORED.

T first sight of the brute, notwithstanding its strangely monstrous appearance, Henry had really mistaken it for a man; but a moment's reflection convinced him that he was looking upon an ape instead of a man, and one of such gigantic size as to make him certain it must be the animal spoken of by Saloo under the various appellations of *mias rombi*, *ourang-outang*, and *red gorilla*. Saloo's remarks concerning this ape, and his emphatic warnings, were not at all pleasant to be now recalled. Though brave as a young lion, he looked upon the shaggy monster with fear and trembling. Far less for himself than for his sister; who, being nearer to it, was, of course, in greater peril of an attack. This, indeed, seemed imminent, and his first thought was to rush to the spot and discharge his musket into the monster's face. He was restrained only by seeing that Helen, moved by an instinct of self-preservation, had made an effort to save herself by

gliding round the trunk of the tree, and seeking concealment on its opposite side. At the same time she had prudently ceased her cries; and as the animal did not show any intention of following her, but rather seemed inclined to keep toward the edge of the lake, the boy bethought him that his best course would be not to discharge his musket until the ape should make some hostile demonstration.

Saloo had told them that the brute is not always disposed to commence the attack upon man. If left alone, it will go its own way, except during certain seasons, when the females are fearful for their young offspring. Then they will assail every intruder that comes near, whether man or animal. But when wounded or enraged they will not only act on the defensive, but attack their enemies in the most spiteful and implacable manner.

Remembering these things, and hoping the huge creature might take a peaceful departure from the place, Henry, who had already held his musket at the level, lowered its muzzle, at the same time dropping upon his knees among some tall grass, which, in this attitude, tolerably well concealed him.

He soon saw that he had acted wisely. The hairy monster seemed altogether to ignore the presence of his sister and himself; and as if neither were within a thousand miles of the spot, kept on its course toward the margin of the water. Fortunately for Henry, it went quite another way, which, widening diagonally, did not bring the creature at all near him. It was evidently directing its course toward some liliaceous plants with large succulent stems, which formed a patch or bed, standing in the water, but close to the brink of the lake.

From what Saloo had said, he knew that the ourang-outang subsists chiefly on fruits; but these sometimes failing, it takes to the leaves and shoots of water-plants, found plenteously along the banks of tropical streams and the shores of inland lakes. In all probability there was not enough fruit in the neighborhood to satisfy the hirsute gentleman now passing before their eyes; or else he had a fancy to vary his diet by making a meal upon some simple vegetables. He soon reached the patch of tall water-plants; waded in nearly knee-deep; and then with arms, each of which had the sweep of a mower's scythe, drew in their heads toward him, and with a mouth wide as that of a hippopotamus, cropped off the succulent shoots and flower-stems, and munched them like an ox in the act of chewing its cud.

Seeing the huge hairy creature thus peaceably disposed, and hoping it would for some time continue in this harmless disposition, Henry rose from his kneeling attitude, and glided silently, but swiftly, toward the tree. Joining his sister Helen, he flung his arms around her as he rose erect, and kissed her to chase away the effects of the terrible fright she had sustained.

CHAPTER XXVI.

IN FEAR AND TREMBLING.

THE kiss which Henry gave his little sister was not one of congratulation. He was not yet sure of her safety, or of his own. The hairy monster was still in sight—not more than a hundred yards off—and though apparently busy with his banquet on the tender shoots of the water-plants, might at any moment discontinue it, and spring upon them.

What was the best thing to be done in order to escape him? Run off into the forest, and try to find their father and Saloo? They might go the wrong way, and by so doing make things worse. The great ape itself would soon be returning among the trees, and might meet them in the teeth; there would then be no chance of avoiding an encounter.

To go after Murtagh would be an equally doubtful proceeding; they were ignorant of the direction the ship-carpenter had taken.

Young as they were, a moment's reflection admonished them not to stir from the spot.

But what, then? Cry out, so that the absent ones might hear them? No; for this might also attract the attention of the ourang-outang, and bring it upon them. Besides, Helen had shrieked loudly on the first alarm. If any of the hunters had been within hearing, they would have needed no further signal to tell them that some danger threatened her. If not within hearing, it would be worse than idle for either of them to cry out again. They determined, therefore, to remain silent, and keep to their position, in the hope that either their father, the Malay, or Murtagh, might come to their speedy relief.

But they were prudent enough not to expose themselves to any wandering glance of the red gorilla's. The moment Henry had joined his sister he had hurried her behind the trunk of the tree, and they were now on the side facing toward the forest. There, by looking through the leaves of some orchideous creepers that wreathed the great stem, they could see the dreaded creature without being seen by it. Hand in hand, still trembling, they stood silently and cautiously regarding the gorilla and its movements.

Under other and safer circumstances it would have been a curious and interesting spectacle: this gigantic, human-like ape, stretching forth its hairy arms, each full four feet in length—gathering in the heads of the tall water-plants, and munching them in great mouthfuls, then letting the stalks go and sweeping round to collect a fresh sheaf, at intervals wading a pace or two to reach some that were more tempting to its taste. For several minutes they remained looking at this rare sight, which would have absorbed the attention of the spectators could it have been witnessed in a menagerie.

But they regarded it with fear and awe. Their eyes and ears were at the same time more occupied in looking and listening for some sign that might tell them of the return of their protectors.

Time passed; none was seen, none heard.

A long time passed, and no sound from the forest; no murmur of men's voices, or cry of scared bird, to proclaim that any one was approaching the spot.

The brute was still browsing, but with less apparent voracity. He drew the shoots toward him with a gentler sweep of his arms, selecting only the most succulent. His appetite was on the wane; it was evident he would soon leave off eating and return to his roosting or resting-place. In the forest, of course, though they knew not where. It might be on the tree over their heads, or on one close at hand; or it might be afar off. In any case, they felt that a crisis was approaching.

Both trembled, as they thought how soon they might be face to face with the hideous creature—confronting it, or perhaps enfolded in its long hairy arms. And in such an embrace, how would it fare with them? What chance of escape from it? None! They would be crushed, helpless as flies in the grasp of a gigantic spider. If the creature should come that way, and resolve upon assailing them, one or other, or both of them, would surely be destroyed.

If only one, Henry had fully made up his mind who it should be. The brave boy had determined to sacrifice his own life, if need be, to save his sister. Firmly grasping the great musket, he said:—

"Sister Nell, if it come this way and offer to attack us, you keep out of the scrape. Leave everything to me. Go a good way off when you see me preparing to fire. I shan't draw trigger till it is close up to the muzzle of the gun. Then there'll be no fear of missing it. To miss would only make it all the madder. Saloo said so. If the shot shouldn't kill it right off, don't mind me. The report may be heard, and bring father or some of the others to our assistance. Dear sis, no matter what happens, keep out of the way, and wait till they come up. Promise me you will do so!"

"Henry! I will not leave you. Dear, dear brother, if you should be killed I would not care to live longer. Henry! I will die with you!"

"Don't talk that way, sis. I'm not going to be killed; for I fancy that we can run faster than it can. It don't appear to make much speed—at least along the ground; and I think we might both escape it if we only knew which way it was going to take. At any rate, you do as I say, and leave the rest to me."

While they were thus discussing the course to be pursued—Henry urging his sister to retreat in the event of his being attacked, and Helen tearfully protesting against leaving him—a movement on the part of the mias claimed all their attention. It was not a movement indicating any design to leave the spot where it had been browsing; but rather a start, as if something caused it a surprise. The start was quickly followed by a gesture, not of alarm, but one that plainly betokened anger. Indeed, it spoke audibly of this, being accompanied by a fierce growl, and succeeded by a series of hoarse barkings, just like those of a bull-dog or angry mastiff, whose mouth, confined in a muzzle, hinders him from giving full vent to his anger. At the same time, instead of rising erect, as a human being under similar circumstances would have done, the frightful ape, that had been already in the most upright position possible to it, dropped down upon all fours, which still, however, from the great length of its arms, enabled it to preserve a semi-erect attitude.

With its huge cheek callosities puffed out beyond their natural dimensions—(they far exceed a foot in breadth)—its crested hair thrown forward in a stiff coronal ruff; underneath a pair of eyes, gleaming like two coals of fire, and, further down, its mouth wide agape, displaying two rows of great glistening teeth, it stood—or rather crouched—as if awaiting for the onset of some well-known enemy; a dangerous enemy, but yet not so dangerous that it need be avoided. On the contrary, the attitude now assumed by the red gorilla, as also its voice and gestures, told them that it was affected by no fear, but breathed only fury and defiance.

Why should it fear? Was there any living thing in the forests of Borneo—biped, quadruped, or reptile possessed of sufficient powers to cope with the hairy colossus now before their eyes, which seemed to partake of the characters of all three, and twice the strength of any of them individually? Saloo had said there was none.

But it was not from the forests of Borneo its enemy was to come. Out of its waters was approaching the antagonist that had caused it to assume its attitude of angry defiance; and the spectators now saw this antagonist in the shape of an enormous lizard—a crocodile larger than they had ever seen before.

In the long dark form, horizontally shooting between the stems of the water-plants, causing the

WATCHING THE GORILLA.

Page 175

red gorilla to utter such angry cries and make such furious gestures, they recognized another great *gavial*, the dreaded crocodile of the East Indian rivers and lagoons.

CHAPTER XXVII.

A SPECTACLE RARELY SEEN.

WHEN the huge reptile first unfolded itself to their view, it was already close to the spot where the ourang-outang, knee-deep in the water, stood awaiting it. They naturally expected to see the land animal effect a retreat from an antagonist even more formidable-looking than itself.

And in reality it did give ground at first; but only for a few long scrambling strides, made as much on its arms as legs—just far enough to place itself high and dry upon the bank. There it came to a stop, and stood firmly facing the foe.

They now perceived the truth of what Saloo had been telling them: that there is no animal in all Borneo, either in its forests or its rivers, of which the mias feels fear. Certainly there is none more to be dreaded than the gavial crocodile; yet the great ape, judging by its present attitude, was in no sense afraid of it. Had it been so, it would have retreated into the woods, where, by climbing a tree, it might easily have shunned the encounter. Even if it had retired a little upon *terra firma*, the amphibious animal would not have thought of following it, and it could at once have avoided the conflict, if desirous of doing so. On the contrary, it seemed rather to court it; for not only did it take a firm stand on the approach of the saurian, but continued to emit its hoarse cough and bark, which, as we have said before, closely resembled the growlings of an angry mastiff with his jaws held half-shut by the traps of a muzzle. At the same time it struck the ground repeatedly with its fore-paws, tearing up grass and weeds, and flinging them spitefully toward the crocodile, and into its very teeth, as if provoking the latter to the attack.

Undismayed, the scaly reptile continued to advance. Neither the strange noises nor the violent gesticulations of its four-handed enemy seemed to have any effect upon it. To all appearance, nothing could terrify the gigantic saurian. Confident in its great size and strength—above all, in the thick impenetrable skin that covered its body like a coat of shale armor—conscious of being so defended, the crocodile also believed that there was no living thing in all the land of Borneo, or in its waters either, that could withstand its terrible onslaught. It therefore advanced to the attack with no idea of danger to itself, but only the thought of seizing upon the half-crouching, half-upright form that had intruded upon its domain, and which possibly appeared to it only a weak human being—a poor Dyak, like some of its former victims.

In this respect it was wofully deceiving itself; and the slight retreat made by the mias toward the dry land no doubt further misled its assailant. The reptile paused for a moment, lest the retreat should be continued, at the same time sinking its body beneath the water as low as the depth would allow.

Remaining motionless for a few seconds, and seeing that its victim was not only not going any further, but maintained its defiant attitude, the gavial crawled silently and cautiously on till the reeds no longer concealed it. Then suddenly rising on its strong fore-arms, it bounded forward—aiding the movement by a stroke of its immense tail—and launched the whole length of its body on the bank, its huge jaws flying agape as they came in contact with the shaggy skin of its intended prey. For an instant of time its snout was actually buried in the long red hair of the gorilla, and the spectators expected to see the latter grasped between its jaws and dragged into the lake.

They were even congratulating themselves on the chance of thus getting rid of it, when a movement on the part of the mias warned them they were not to be so conveniently disembarrassed of its dangerous proximity. That movement was a leap partly to one side, and partly upward into the air. It sprang so high as completely to clear the head of its assailant, and so far horizontally, that when it came to the ground again, it was along the extended body of the crocodile, midway between its head and its tail. Before the unwieldy reptile could turn to confront it, the ape made a second spring, this time alighting upon the gavial's back, just behind his shoulders. There straddling, and taking a firm hold with its thick short legs, it threw its long arms forward over the crocodile's shoulder-blades, as with the intent to throttle it. And now commenced a struggle between the two monstrous creatures—a conflict strange and terrible—such as could only be seen in the depths of a Bornean or Sumatran forest, in the midst of those wild solitudes where man rarely makes his way. And even in such scenes but rarely witnessed; and only by the lone Dyak hunter straying along the banks of some solitary stream, or threading the mazes of the jungle-grown swamp or lagoon.

On the part of the crocodile the strife consisted simply in a series of endeavors to dismount the hairy rider who clung like a saddle to its back. To effect this purpose, it made every effort in its power; turning about upon its belly as upon a pivot; snapping its jaws till they cracked like pistol shots; lashing the ground with its long vertebrated tail, till the grass and weeds were swept off as if cut with the blade of a scythe; twisting and wriggling in every possible direction.

All to no purpose. The ape held on as firmly as a Mexican to a restive mule, one of its fore-arms clutching the shoulder-blade of the reptile, while the other was constantly oscillating in the air, as if searching for something to seize upon.

For what purpose it did this, the spectators could not at first tell. It was not long, however, before they discovered its intention. All at once the disengaged arm made a long clutch forward and grasped the upper jaw of the gavial. During the struggle this had been frequently wide agape, almost pointing vertically upward, as is customary with reptiles of the lizard kind, the singular conformation of the cervical vertebræ enabling them to open their jaws thus widely. One might have supposed that, in thus taking hold, the gorilla had got its hand into a terrible trap, and that in another instant its fingers would be caught between the quickly-closing teeth of the saurian, and snapped off like pipe-stems, or the tender shoots of a head of celery. The inexperienced and youthful spectators expected some such result; but not so the cunning old man-monkey, who knew what he was about; for, once he had gained a good hold upon the upper jaw, at its narrowest part, near the snout, he made up his mind that those bony counterparts, now asunder, should never come together again. To make quite sure of this, he bent himself to the last supreme effort. Supporting his knees firmly against the shoulders of the saurian, and bending his thick muscular arms to the extent of their great strength, he was seen to give one grand wrench. There was a crashing sound, as of a tree torn from its roots, followed by a spasmodic struggle; then the hideous reptile lay extended along the earth, still writhing its body and flirting its tail.

The red gorilla saw that it had accomplished its task; victory was achieved, the danger over, and the hated enemy lay helpless, almost nerveless, in its hairy embrace.

At length, detaching itself from the scaly creature, whose struggles each moment grew feebler and feebler, it sprang to one side, squatted itself on its haunches, and with a hoarse laughter, that resembled the horrid yell of a maniac, triumphantly contemplated the ruin of its prostrate foe!

CHAPTER XXVIII.

STILL TRUSTING IN GOD.

THE reader may suppose the strange conflict we have described to be a thing of the author's imagination. Some will, no doubt, pronounce it a story of the sensational and fabulous kind—in short, a "sailor's yarn." So may it seem to those who give but little attention to the study of nature. To the naturalist, however, this chapter of animal life and habits will cause no astonishment; for he will know it to be a true one; and that the spectacle described, although perhaps not one coming every day under the eye of man, and especially civilized man, has nevertheless been witnessed by the inhabitants of the recesses of the Bornean forest.

Ask any old Bornean bee-hunter, and he will tell you just such a tale as the above: adding that the ourang-outang, or red gorilla, which he calls *mias*, is a match, and more than a match, for any animal it may encounter in forest or jungle: and that the only two creatures which dare attack it are the crocodile and the great *ular* or *python*, the latter a serpent of the boa-constrictor kind, with one of which our castaways had already formed acquaintance. But the Bornean bee-hunter, usually a Dyak, will also tell you that in these conflicts the red gorilla is the victor, though each of the two great reptile antagonists that attack it is often thirty feet in length, with a girth almost equalling its own. Only fancy a snake ten yards long, and a lizard the same; either of which would reach from end to end of the largest room in which you may be seated, or across the street in which you may be walking! You will seldom find such specimens in our museums; for they are not often encountered by our naturalists or secured by our travellers. But take my word for it, there are such serpents and such lizards in existence, ay, and much larger ones. They may be found not only in the tropical isles of the Orient, but in the Western world, in the lagoons and forests of Equatorial America. Many of the "sailor's yarns" of past times, which we have been accustomed so flippantly to discredit, on account of their appearing rather tough, have under the light of recent scientific exploration been proved true.

And although some of them may seem to be incorporated in this narrative, under the guise of mere romance, the reader need not on this account think himself misled, or treat them with sublime contempt. If it should ever be his fate or fortune to make a tour through the East Indian Archipelago, he will cease to be incredulous.

Henry Redwood and his sister Helen had no such tranquil reflections, as they stood under the shadow of the great tree, concealing themselves behind its trunk, and watching the terrible conflict between the two huge creatures, both in their eyes equally hideous.

Giving way to an instinct of justice, they would have taken sides with the party assailed and against the assailant. But, under the circumstances, their leanings were the very reverse; for in the triumphant conqueror they saw a continuance of their own danger; whereas, had the amphibious animal been victorious, this would have been at an end. The strife now terminated, they stood trembling and uncertain as ever.

The crocodile, although crushed, and no longer dangerous for any offensive manœuvre, was not killed. Its body still writhed and wriggled upon the ground; though its movements were but the agonized efforts of mortal pain, excited convulsively, and each moment becoming feebler.

And the red gorilla stood near, squatted on its haunches; at intervals tossing its long hairy arms around its head, and giving utterance to that strange coughing laughter, as if it would never leave off exulting over the victory it had achieved.

How long was this spectacle to last? It was sufficiently horrid for the spectators to desire its speedy termination.

And yet they did not; they were in hopes it might continue till a voice coming from the forest, or the tread of a foot, would tell them that help was near.

Tremblingly but attentively they listened. They heard neither one nor the other—neither voice nor footstep. Now and then came the note of a bird or the cry of some four-footed creature prowling through the glades; but not uttered in accents of alarm. The hunters must have wandered far in their search for game. They might not return in time.

Again Henry bethought him of firing the musket to give them a signal. But even if heard, it might not have this effect. They knew that he was able to hold and handle the great gun, and might think some bird or animal had come near and tempted him to take a shot at it.

On the other hand, the report would strike upon the ears of the mias, might distract it from the triumph in which it was indulging, and bring it to the spot where they were standing. Then, with an empty gun in his hand, what defence could the youth make, either for himself or for his sister?

To fire the gun would never do. Better leave the trigger unpulled, and trust to Providence for protection.

And then, as the brave boy reflected on the many dangers through which they had passed, and how they had always been delivered by some fortunate interposition, he knew it must be the hand of Providence, and was content to rely upon it again.

He said so to his little sister, whispering consolation, as with one hand he drew her close to him, the other resting upon the musket. And Helen whispered back a pious response, as she nestled upon the breast of her brother.

A moment more, and the faith of both was submitted to a severe trial.

The red gorilla, after gloating for a long time over the agonized contortions of its disabled enemy, seemed at length satisfied that it was disabled to death, and facing toward the forest, showed signs of an intention to take its departure from the spot.

Now came the crisis for Henry and Helen. Which way would the animal take?

They had not time to exchange question and answer—scarce time even to shape them in their thoughts—when they saw the red satyr turn to the tree behind which they were standing, and come directly toward them.

CHAPTER XXIX.

A CAPTIVE CARRIED ALOFT.

E are lost!" were the words that rushed from Henry Redwood's lips. They came involuntarily; for, as soon as said, he regretted them, seeing how much they added to the alarm of his sister. It was a crisis in which she needed rather to be inspired to confidence by words of encouragement.

They were said, however, and he could not recall them. He had no time to speak of anything, or to think of what course they should now pursue. Coming straight toward the tree with an awkward, shambling, but speedy gait withal, the monster would soon reach the spot where they stood. Its movements showed it to be in a state of excitement—the natural consequence of its late conflict with the crocodile. If seen, they would come in for a share of its anger, already roused.

If seen! They were almost sure of being seen. They were endeavoring to avoid it by keeping on the other side of the tree, and screening themselves among the parasitical plants. But the concealment was slight, and would not avail them if the animal should pass the trunk and look around after passing. And now it was making straight for the tree, apparently with a design of ascending it.

At this crisis Henry once more bethought him of running away and taking Helen with him. He now regretted not having done so sooner. Even to be lost in the forest would have been a less danger than that which now threatened them.

A glance told him it would be too late. There was an open space beyond and all around the trunk behind which they had taken shelter. Should they attempt to escape, the ape would be certain of seeing them before they could get under cover of the woods, and, as they supposed, might easily overtake them in their flight.

Another tree was near, connecting that under which they stood with the adjoining forest. But it was in a side direction, and they would be seen before reaching it. There was no alternative but to risk a chase, or stay where they were, and take the chances of not being seen by the horrid creature that was approaching. They chose the latter.

Silently they stood, hands clasped and close to the stem of the tree, on the side opposite to that on which the gorilla was advancing. They no longer saw it; for now they dared not look around the trunk, or even peep through the leaves of the orchids, lest their faces might betray them.

After all, the ape might pass into the forest without observing them. If it did, the danger would be at an end; if not, the brave boy had summoned up all his energies to meet and grapple with it. He held the loaded musket in his hand, ready at a moment's notice to raise it to the level and fire into the face of the red-haired satyr.

They waited in breathless silence, though each could hear the beating of the other's heart.

It was torture to stand thus uncertain; and, as if to continue it, the animal was a long time in getting to the tree. Had it stopped, or turned off some other way?

Henry was tempted to peep round the trunk and satisfy himself. He was about to do this, when a scratching on the other side fell upon their ears. It was the claws of the mias rasping against the bark. The next moment the sound seemed higher up, and they were made aware that the creature was ascending the tree.

Henry was already congratulating himself on this event. The ape might go up without seeing them; and as the tree was a very tall one, with a thick head of foliage and matted creepers, once among these, it might no longer think of looking down. Then they could steal away unobserved, and, keeping at a safe distance, await the return of the hunters.

At this moment, however, an incident arose that

interfered with this desirable programme, in an instant changing the position of everything that promised so well into a sad and terrible catastrophe.

It was Murtagh who caused, though innocently, the lamentable diversion.

The ship-carpenter, returning from his excursion, had just stumbled upon the crocodile where it lay upon the shore of the lake, which, though helpless to return to its proper element, was not yet dead. With jaw torn and dislocated, it was still twisting its body about in the last throes of the death-struggle.

Not able to account for the spectacle of ruin thus presented, it caused the Irishman much surprise, not unmingled with alarm—the latter increasing as he looked toward the tree where Henry and Helen had been left, and saw they were no longer there.

Had he prudently held his peace, perhaps all might have been well; but, catching sight of the huge hairy monster ascending the trunk, the thought flashed across his mind that the young people had been already destroyed, perhaps devoured, by it; and, giving way to this terrible fancy, he uttered a dread cry of despair.

It was the worst thing he could have done; for, despite the discouraging tone of his voice, it seemed joyful to those crouching in concealment; and, yielding to an instinct that they were now saved by the presence of a stanch protector, they rushed from their ambuscade, and in so doing discovered themselves to the ourang-outang.

Its eyes were upon them—dark, demon-like orbs, that seemed to scintillate sparks of fire. The gorilla had only gone up the trunk to the height of about twenty feet, when the cry of the alarmed ship-carpenter brought its ascent to a sudden stop; then, bringing its body half round, and looking below, it saw the children.

As if connecting them with the enemy it had just conquered, its angry passions seemed to rekindle; and once more giving utterance to that strange barking cough, it glided down the tree, and made direct for the one who was nearest.

As ill luck would have it, this chanced to be the little Helen, altogether defenceless and unarmed. Murtagh, still shouting, rushed to the rescue; while Henry, with his musket raised to his shoulder, endeavored to get between the ape and its intended victim, so that he could fire right into the face of the assailant, without endangering the life of his sister.

He would have been in time had the gun proved true, which it did not. It was an old flint musket, and the priming had got damp during their journey through the moist tropical forest. As he pulled trigger, there was not even a flash in the pan; and although he instinctively grasped the gun by its barrel, and, using it as a club, commenced belaboring the hairy giant over the head, his blows were of no more avail than if directed against the trunk of the tree itself.

Once, twice, three times the butt of the gun descended upon the skull of the satyr, protected by its thick shock of coarse red hair; but before a fourth blow could be given, the ape threw out one of its immense arms, and carrying it round in a rapid sweep, caught the form of the girl in its embrace, and then, close hugging her against its hairy breast, commenced re-ascending the tree.

Shouts and shrieks were of no avail to detain the horrid abductor. Nor yet the boy's strength, exerted to its utmost. His strength alone; for Murtagh was not yet up. Henry seized the gorilla's leg, and clung to it as long as ever he could. He was dragged several feet up the trunk; but a kick from the gorilla shook him off, and he fell, stunned and almost senseless, to the earth.

On recovering his feet and his senses, he looked above. He had been unconscious only for an instant, and throughout his swoon had heard Helen's continued shrieks like voices in a dreadful dream. These now directed him; and at the first glance on high, he saw his sister still held in the hug of the horrid creature, which was moving onward and upward, as if determined on taking her to the very top of the tree.

CHAPTER XXX.

WHAT WILL BECOME OF HER?

IT would be impossible to paint the despair that wrung her brother's heart, as he stood with upturned face and eyes bent upon a scene in which he had no longer the power to take part.

Not much less intense was the agonized emotion of Murtagh; for little Helen was almost as dear to the Irishman as if she had been his own daughter.

Neither could have any other thought than that the child was lost beyond hope of recovery. She would either be torn to pieces by the claws of the monster, or by its great yellow teeth, already displayed to their view, and flung in mangled fragments to the ground. They actually stood for some time in expectation of seeing this sad catastrophe; and it would be vain to attempt any description of their emotions.

It was no relief when the two hunters came up, as they did at that instant, on their return from the chase. Their approach for the last two o three hundred yards had been hastened into a run by the shrieks of Helen and the shouts of Henry and Murtagh. Their arrival only added two new figures to the tableau of distress, and two voices to its expression.

The ape could still be seen through the foliage ascending to the top of the tree; but Captain Redwood felt that the rifle he held in his hands, though sure of aim and fatal in effect, was of no more use than if it had been a piece of wood.

Saloo had the same feeling in regard to his blow-gun. The rifle might send a deadly bullet through the skull of the gorilla, and the latter pierce its body with an arrow that would carry a quick-spreading poison through its veins.

But to what purpose, even though they could be certain of killing it? Its death would be also the death of the child. She was still living, and apparently unhurt; for they could see her moving, and hear her voice, as she was carried onward and upward in that horrible embrace.

Captain Redwood dared not send a bullet nor Saloo an arrow. Slight as the chances were of saving the girl, either would have made them slighter. A successful shot of the rifle or puff of the blow-gun would be as fatal to the abducted as the abductor; and the former, with or without the latter, would be certain to fall to the foot of the tree. It was a hundred feet sheer from the point which the ape had attained to the ground. The child would not only be killed, but crushed to a shapeless mass.

Ah me! what a terrible scene for her father! What a spectacle for him to contemplate!

And as he stood in unutterable agony, his companions gathered around, all helpless and irresolute as to how they should act, they saw the ape suddenly change his direction, and move outward from the trunk of the tree along one of its largest limbs. This trended off in a nearly horizontal direction, at its end interlocking with a limb of the neighboring tree, which stretched out as if to shake hands with it.

A distance of more than fifty feet lay between the two trunks, but their branches met in close embrace.

The purpose of the ape was apparent. It designed passing from one to the other, and thence into the depths of the forest.

The design was quickly followed by its execution. As the spectators rushed to the side by which the gorilla was retreating, they saw it lay hold of the interlocking twigs, draw the branch nearer, bridge the space between with its long straggling arm, and then bound from one to the other with the agility of a squirrel.

And this with the use of only one arm, for by the other the child was still carried in the same close hug. Its legs acted as arms, and for travelling through the tree-tops three were sufficient.

On into the heart of the deep foliage of the second tree, and without a pause on into the next; along another pair of counterpart limbs, which, intertwining their leafy sprays and boughs, still further into the forest, all the time bearing its precious burden along with it.

The agonized father ran below, rifle in hand. He might as well have been without one, for all the use he dared to make of it.

And Henry, too, followed with the ship's musket. True, it had missed fire, and the damp priming was still in the pan. Damp or dry, it now mattered not. Saloo's sumpitan was an equally ineffective weapon. Murtagh with his fishing-hooks might as well have thought of capturing the monster with a bait.

On it scrambled from tree to tree, and on ran the pursuers underneath, yet with no thought of being able to stay its course. They were carried forward by the mere mechanical instinct to keep it in sight, with perhaps some slight hope that in the end something might occur—some interruption might arise by which they would be enabled to effect a rescue of the child from its horrible captor.

It was at best but a faint consolation. Nor would they have cherished it, but for their trust in a higher power than their own. Of themselves they knew they could not let or hinder the abductor in its flight.

All felt their own helplessness. But it is just in that supreme moment, when man feels his utter weakness, that his vague trust in a superior Being becomes a devout and perfect faith.

Captain Redwood was not what is usually called a religious man, meaning thereby a strict adherent to the Church, and a regular observer of its ordinances. For all this he was a firm believer in the existence of a providential and protecting power.

His exclamations were many, and not very coherent; but their burden was ever a prayer to God for the preservation of his daughter.

"Helen, my child! Helen! What will become of her? O Father! O God, protect her!"

CHAPTER XXXI.

THE PURSUIT ARRESTED.

FROM branch to branch, and tree to tree, the red gorilla continued its swift advance; still bearing with it the little Helen.

From trunk to trunk, the pursuers crawled through the underwood beneath, feeling as helpless as ever.

What was to be the end of this strangely singular pursuit they could not tell, for they had never before—and perhaps no man at any time had—taken part in such a chase, or even heard of one so terrible.

They could offer no conjecture as to what might be its termination; but moved forward mechanically, keeping the gorilla in sight.

Was Helen yet living or was she dead? No cry came from her lips, no word, no sound! Had the life been crushed out of her body by the pressure of that strong muscular arm, twined round her like the limb of an oak? Or was the silence due to temporary loss of feeling?

She might well have swooned away in such a situation; and her father, struggling with faint hopes, would have been glad to think this was indeed the case.

No signs could be gained from what they heard, and none from what they saw. They were now passing through the very depth of the forest—a tropical forest, with the trees meeting overhead, and not a speck of sky visible through the interwoven branches, loaded with their thick festoons of leaves and lianas.

They were gliding through dense arcades, lit up with just sufficient sunshine to wear the sombre shadows of a dusky twilight. There were even places where the retreating form of the ape could not have been distinguishable in the obscurity, but for the white drapery of the child's dress, now torn into shreds, and flaunting like streamers behind it. These luckily served as a beacon to guide them on through the gloom.

Now and then the chase led them into less shady depths, where the sunlight fell more freely through the leafy screen above. At such points they could obtain a better view, both of the red abductor and its captive.

But even then only a glimpse—the speed at which the gorilla was going, as well as the foliage that intervened, preventing any lengthened observation.

Nor were the pursuers at any time able to get sight of the child's face. It appeared to be turned toward the animal's breast, her head buried in its coarse shaggy hair, with which her own tresses were mingled in strange contrast.

Even her form could not be clearly distinguished. As far as they could decide by their occasional glimpses, they thought she was still alive. The brute did not seem to treat her with any malevolent violence. Only in a rude uncouth way; which, however, might suffice to cause the death of one so young and frail.

To depict the feelings of her father, under such circumstances, would be a task the most eloquent pen could not successfully attempt. Agony like his can never be described. Language possesses not the power. There are thoughts which lie too deep for words; passions whose expression defies the genius of the artist or the poet.

Perhaps he was hindered from realizing the full measure of his bereavement during the first moments of the pursuit. The excitement of the chase, and the incidents attending it—the hope still remaining that some chance would arise in their favor—the certainty, soon ascertained, that they could keep up with the ape, which, despite its agility in the trees, cannot outstrip a man pursuing it along the ground,—all these circumstances had hitherto withheld him from giving way to utter despair.

But the time had come when even these slight supports were to fail.

It was when they arrived upon the brink of a lagoon, and a water-surface gleamed before their eyes; reflected by a daylight that struggled dimly down through the tops of the tall trees.

The trees rose out of the water, their trunks wide apart, but their branches intermingling.

The path of our pursuers was interrputed—they saw it at once—but that of the pursued seemed continuous as before.

They were arrested suddenly on the brink of the lagoon, apparently with no chance of proceeding farther. They saw the red gorilla still climbing among the trees, with the white drapery streaming behind it.

Soon they saw it not—only heard the crackle of twigs, and the swishing recoil of the branches, as its huge body swung from tree to tree.

The monster was now out of sight, along with its victim—a victim, in very truth, whether living or dead!

But for the support of Murtagh and Saloo, Captain Redwood would have fallen to the earth. In their arms he sobbed and gasped,—

"Helen! my child, Helen! What will become of her? O Father! O God, protect her!"

CHAPTER XXXII.

LISTENING IN DESPAIR.

FOR some seconds Captain Redwood was powerless in a frenzy of despair. Henry was equally overcome by grief truly agonizing. It was to both father and son a moment of the most unutterable anguish.

Helen, the dear daughter and sister, carried out of their sight, apparently beyond reach of pursuit ! And in the arms of a hideous creature which was neither wholly man nor wholly beast, but combined the worst attributes of each.

Perhaps she was already dead within the loathsome embrace—her tender body soon to be torn to pieces, or tossed from the top of some tall tree; to be crushed and mangled on the earth, or thrown with a plunge into the cold dark waters of that dismal lagoon, never more to be seen or heard of.

These were horrid thoughts and hideous images which rushed rapidly through their minds as they stood in the sombre shadow, picturing to themselves her too probable fate. It was no longer a question about her life.

They knew, or believed, her to be dead. They only thought of what was to become of her body; what chance there might be of recovering and giving it the sacred rights of sepulture. Even this slight consolation occupied the mind of the distracted father.

The Malay, well acquainted with the habits of the great man-ape, could give no answer. He only knew that the child's body would not be eaten up by it; since the red gorilla is never known to feed upon flesh—fruit and vegetables being its only diet.

The whole thing was perplexing him, as an occurrence altogether unusual. He had known of people being killed and torn to pieces by the animal in its anger; but never of one being carried up into the trees.

Usually these animals will not volunteer an attack upon man, and are only violent when assailed. Then, indeed, are they terrible in their strength as in their ferocity.

The one now encountered must have been infuriated by its fight with the crocodile; and coming straight from the encounter, had in some way connected the children with its conquered enemy. Murtagh's shout might have freshly incensed it; or, what to Saloo seemed more probable than all, the seizure of the child might be a wild freak suddenly striking the brain of the enraged satyr.

He had heard of such eccentricities on the part of the ourang-outang, and there is a belief among the Dyak hunters that the mias sometimes goes *mad*, just as men do.

This reasoning did not take place on the edge of the lagoon, nor any discussion of such questions. They were thoughts that had been expressed during the pursuit, at no time hurried. The captain and his companions had easily kept pace with the pursued, while passing through the dry forest; and time enough was allowed them to think and talk of many things.

Now that they could no longer follow, scarce a word was exchanged between them. Their emotions were too sad for utterance, otherwise than by exclamations which spoke only of despair.

It was well they were silent, for it gave Saloo the opportunity of listening. Ever since the ape had passed from their sight, his ear had been keenly anxious to catch every sound, as he still entertained a hope of being able to trace its passage through the trees.

Thoroughly conversant with the animal's habits, he knew that it must have an abiding-place—a nest. This might be near at hand. The proximity of the lagoon almost convinced him that it was so.

The mias makes a temporary roost for his repose

anywhere it may be wandering—constructing it in a few moments, by breaking off the branches and laying them crosswise on a forked limb; but Saloo was aware that, for its permanent residence, it builds a much more elaborate nest, and this, too, always over water or marshy ground, where its human enemy cannot conveniently follow it.

Moreover, it chooses for the site of its dwelling a low tree or bush with umbrageous boughs, and never retires among the taller trees of the forest.

This it does to avoid exposure to the chill winds, and the inconvenience of being shaken to and fro during storms or typhoons.

With all this knowledge in his memory, the Malay had conceived a hope that the monster's nest might not be far off, and they would still be able to follow and find it—not to rescue the living child, but recover her dead body.

Keenly and attentively he listened to every sound that came back through the water-forest—cautioning the others to be silent. A caution scarce needed, for they too stood listening, still as death, with hushed voices, and hearts only heard in their dull sad beatings.

But for a short time were they thus occupied; altogether not more than five minutes. They still detected the crackling of branches which indicated the passage of the ape through the tree-tops.

All at once these sounds suddenly ceased, or

14

rather were they drowned out by sounds louder and of a very different intonation. It was a chorus of cries, in which barking, grunting, growling, coughing, cachinnation, and the squalling of children seemed all to have a share. There were evidently more than one individual contributing to this strange *fracas* of the forest; and the noises continued to come apparently from the same place.

If the hateful mias were one of the hoarse choristers, it had evidently paused in its career. This was the conjecture, or rather the conviction, of Saloo.

"Allah be thank!" he exclaimed, in a subdued tone. "He home at lass. Him family makee welcome. If lilly Helen no live, we get body—and we hab revenge."

Saloo's words, offering such poor consolation, fell with sad effect on the ears of his listeners. He saw this, and added:

"Ledwud no glieve, cappen. Maybe chile be live yet. Maybe mias no killee after all. Trust we in Allah, what you Inglees people callee God. Who know he yet help us!"

These last words came like a renewal of life to the despairing father. He started on hearing them; fresh hope had sprung up in his breast, at the thought that his beloved child might yet be alive, and that a chance of rescuing her might still be possible.

"In thy mercy, O God, grant it may be so!" were the words that fell from his lips; Murtagh, with equal fervor, saying "Amen!"

CHAPTER XXXIII.

STRIKING OUT.

NSPIRED to renewed energy, Captain Redwood rushed to the edge of the lagoon, with the view of ascertaining its depth, and seeing whether it might possibly be waded.

He soon discovered that it could not. In less than ten paces from the edge he was up to the arm-pits, and from thence it seemed to deepen still more abruptly. Another step forward, and the water rose over his shoulders, the bottom still sloping downward. The lagoon was evidently impassable.

He drew back despairingly, though not to return to the shore. He stood facing the centre of the lagoon, whence still came the strange noises: though scarce so loud or varied as before, they did not appear to be any more distant. Whatever creatures were making them, it was evident they were stationary, either in the trees or upon the ground. They did not sound as if they came from on high; but this might be a deception, caused by the influence of the water. One of the voices bore a singular resemblance to that of a child. It could not be Helen's; it more resembled the squalling of an infant. Saloo knew what it was. In the plaintive tones he recognized the scream of a young ourang-outang.

It was a proof his conjecture was true, and that the mias had reached its home.

All the more anxious was Captain Redwood to reach the spot whence the sounds proceeded. Something like a presentiment had entered his mind that there was still a hope, and that his child lived and might be rescued.

Even if torn, injured, disfigured for life, she might survive. Any sort of life, so long as she could be recovered; and if she could not be restored, at least she might breathe her last breath in his arms. Even that would be easier to bear than the thought that she had gone to rest in the grasp of the hirsute gorilla, with its hideous offspring grinning and gibbering around her.

The lagoon could not be waded on foot; but a good swimmer might cross it. The captain was an experienced and accomplished swimmer. The voices came from no great distance—certainly not above half a mile. On one occasion he had accomplished a league in a rough sea! There could be no difficulty in doing as much on the smooth, tranquil water of that tree-shaded lake.

He had opened his arms and prepared to strike out, when a thought stayed him. Saloo, who had waded to his side, also arrested him by laying a hand on his shoulder.

"You try swimmee, cappen, no good without weapon; we both go togedder—muss take gun, sumpitan, kliss, else no chance killee mias."

It was the thought that had occurred to Captain Redwood himself.

"Yes, you are right, Saloo. I must take my rifle, but how am I to keep it dry?—there's not time to make a raft."

"No raff need, cappen; givee me you gun—Saloo swim single-hand well as two; he cally the gun."

Captain Redwood knew it to be true that Saloo, as he said, could swim with one hand as well as he himself with both.

He was a Malay, to whom swimming in the water is almost as natural as walking upon the land. His old pilot could scarcely have been drowned if he had been flung into the sea twenty miles from shore.

He at once yielded to Saloo's counsel; and both hastily returned to the edge of the lagoon to make preparations.

These did not occupy long. The captain threw

off some of his clothes, stowed his powder-flask and some bullets in the crown of his hat, which he fastened firmly on his head. He retained a knife —intended in case of necessity—to be carried between his teeth, giving his gun to Saloo.

The Malay, having less undressing to do, had already completed the arrangements. On the top of his turban, safely secured by a knotting of his long black hair, he had fastened his bamboo quiver of poisoned arrows; while his kris—with which a Malay under no circumstances thinks of parting— lay along his thigh, kept in position by the waist-strap used in suspending his *sarong*. With his sumpitan and the captain's gun in his left hand, he was ready to take the water. Not another moment was lost; the voices of the ourangs seemed to be calling them; and plunging through the shallow, they were soon out in deep water, and striking steadily but rapidly, silently but surely, toward the centre of the lagoon.

Henry and Murtagh remained on the shore looking after them. The ship-carpenter was but an indifferent swimmer, and the youth was not strong enough to have swam half a mile. It was doubtful if either could have reached the spot where the apes seemed to have made their rendezvous. And if so, they would have been too exhausted to have rendered any service in case of a sudden conflict.

The brave Irishman, devoted to his old skipper, and Henry, anxious to share his father's fate, would have made the attempt; but Captain Redwood restrained them, directing both to await his return.

They stood close to the water's edge, following the swimmers with their eyes, and with prayers for their success, scarcely uttered in words, but fervently felt; Murtagh, according to the custom of his country and creed, sealing the petition by making the sign of the cross.

CHAPTER XXXIV.

SWIMMING IN SHADOW.

SILENTLY and swiftly the two swimmers continued their course through the shadowy aisles of the forest. Twilight, almost darkness, was above and around them; for the trees meeting overhead caused an obscurity sombre as night itself. No ray of sunlight ever danced upon the surface of that dismal lagoon.

They would have lost their way, had not the noises guided them. Should these be discontinued, their exertions might be all in vain.

They thought of this as they proceeded, and reflected also on the course to be adopted when they reached the rendezvous of the gorillas. Supposing there could be no footing found, how were they to use either gun or sumpitan?

The question passed between them in a whisper as they swam side by side. Neither knew how to answer it.

Saloo only expressed a hope that they might get upon the limb of a tree near enough to send a bullet or arrow into the body of the mias, and terminate his career.

There seemed no other chance, and they swam on, keeping it before their minds.

About the direction they had no difficulty whatever. Although the surface of the water was of inky blackness, from the shadowing trees above, and the huge trunks standing out of it now and then forced them into an occasional deviation, they advanced without any great difficulty.

They swam around the tree trunks, and guided by the voices of the gorillas, easily regained their course. The noises were no longer sharp screams or hoarse coughs, but a kind of jabbering jargon, as if the apes were engaged in a family confabulation.

The swimmers at length arrived so near, that they no longer felt any fear about finding the way to the place where the reunion of the *quadrumana* was being held; and which could not be more than a hundred yards distant.

Silently gliding through the water, the eyes of both peered intently forward, in an endeavor to pierce the obscurity, and, if possible discover some low limb of a tree, or projecting buttress, on which they might find a foothold. They had good hope of success, for they had seen many such since starting from the shore. Had rest been necessary, they might have obtained it more than once by grasping a branch above, or clinging to one of the great trunks, whose gnarled and knotted sides would have afforded sufficient support.

But they were both strong swimmers, and needed no rest. There was none for the bereaved father— could be none—till he should reach the termination of their strange enterprise, and know what was to be its result.

As they swam onward, now proceeding with increased caution, their eyes scanning the dark surface before them, both all of a sudden and simultaneously came to a stop. It was just as if something underneath the water had laid hold of them by the legs, checking them at the same instant of time.

And something *had* impeded their farther progress, but not from behind. In front was the obstruction, which proved to be a bank of earth, that, though under the water, rose within a few inches of its surface. The breast of each swimmer had struck against it, the shock raising them into a half-erect attitude, from which they had no need to return to the horizontal. On the contrary, they now rose upon their feet, which they felt to be resting on a firm, hard bottom.

Standing in pleased surprise, they could better survey the prospect before them; and after a minute spent in gazing through the gloom, they saw that dry land was close to the spot where they had been so abruptly arrested.

It appeared only a low-lying islet, scarce rising above the level of the lagoon, and of limited extent—only a few rods in superficial area. It was thickly covered with trees; but, unlike those standing in the water, which were tall and with single stems, those upon the islet were supported by many trunks, proclaiming them to be some species of the Indian fig or *banyan*.

One near the centre, from its greater width and more numerous supporting pillars, seemed the patriarch of the tribe; and to this their eyes were especially directed. For out of its leafy shadows came the strange sounds which had hitherto guided them.

Among its branches, without any doubt, the red gorilla had his home; and there he would be found in the bosom of his family.

Grasping his gun, and whispering to Saloo to follow him, Captain Redwood started toward the tree so clearly indicated as the goal of their expedition.

CHAPTER XXXV.

THE FAMILY AT HOME.

SOON after the intended assailants stood among the rooted branches of the banyan. The gloom underneath its umbrageous branches was deepened by what appeared to be an immense scaffolding constructed near the top of the tree, and extending far out along the horizontal limbs.

Saloo at once recognized the permanent nest or roosting-place of a *mias rombi*—such as he had often seen in the forests of Sumatra, where the same, or a closely allied species, has its home.

The tree was not a tall one, but low and wide-spreading; while the broad platform-like nest, formed by interwoven branches, upon which lay a thick layer of grass and leaves, was not more than twenty feet above the surface of the earth.

The obscurity which prevailed around favored their stealthy approach; and like a pair of spectres gliding through the upright pillars, Captain Red wood and his old pilot at length found a position favorable for a survey of the platform erected by the gorilla.

The father's heart was filled with strange indescribable emotions, as with eye keenly bent he stood upon a projecting branch, that brought his head on a level with this curious structure.

There he saw a scene which stirred his soul to its deepest depths.

His daughter, appearing snow-white amid the gloom, was lying upon the scaffold, her golden hair dishevelled, her dress torn into ribbons—portions of it detached and scattered about.

To all appearance she was dead; for, scanning her with the earnest anxious glance of a keen solicitude, he could not detect any movement either in body or limbs; and it was too dark for him to tell whether her eyes were open or closed.

But he had now very little hope. He was indeed too certain they were closed in the sleep of death.

Around her were assembled three human-like forms, monstrous withal, and all alike covered with a coating of red hair, thick, long, and shaggy. They were of different sizes, and in the largest one he recognized the abductor of his child.

The second in size, whose form proclaimed it to be a female, was evidently the wife of the huge man-ape; while the little creature about eighteen inches in height—though a perfect miniature likeness of its parents—was the infant whose squalling had contributed more than anything else to guide them through the shades of the lagoon.

The old male, perhaps suffering fatigue from its fight with the crocodile, as well as from the chase he had sustained, crouched upon the scaffold, seemingly asleep.

The other two were still in motion, the mother at intervals seizing her hairy offspring, and grotesquely caressing it; then letting it go free to dance fantastically around the recumbent form of the unconscious captive child. This it did, amusing itself by now and then tearing off a strip of the girl's dress, either with its claws or teeth.

It was a spectacle wild, weird, altogether indescribable; and by Captain Redwood not to be looked upon a moment longer than was necessary to embrace its details.

Having satisfied himself, he raised his rifle to fire upon the family party, intending first to aim at the father, whose death he most desired, and who living would no doubt prove by far the most dangerous antagonist.

In another instant his bullet would have sped toward the breast of the sleeping giant, but for Saloo, who, grasping his arm, restrained him.

"Tay, cappen," said the Malay in a whisper; "leave me kill em. Sumpit bettel dun bullet.

De gun makee noise—wake old mias up, an' may be no killee em. De upas poison bettel. It go silent—quick. See how Saloo slay dem all tlee!"

There was something in Saloo's suggestions which caused Captain Redwood to ground his rifle and reflect. His reflections quickly ended in his giving place to his old pilot, and leaving the latter to work out the problem in his own way.

Stepping up to the branch assigned to him, which commanded a view of the spectacle so torturing to his master, the Malay took a brief glance at the scene—only a very brief one. It enabled him to select the first victim for his envenomed shaft, the same which Captain Redwood had destined to receive the leaden missile from his gun.

Bringing to his mouth the sumpitan, in whose tube he had already placed one of his poisoned arrows, and compressing the trumpet-shaped embouchure against his lips, he gave a puff that sent the shaft on its deadly way with such velocity, that even in clear daylight its exit could only have been detected like a spark from a flint.

In the obscurity that shrouded the gorilla's roost, nothing at all was seen, and nothing heard; for the sumpit is as silent on its message as the wing of an owl when beating through the twilight.

True, there was something heard, though it was not the sound of the arrow.

Only a growl from the great red gorilla, that had

felt something sting him, and on feeling it threw up his paw to scratch the place, no doubt fancying it to be but the bite of a mosquito or hornet.

The piece of stick broken off by his fingers may have seemed to him rather strange, but not enough so to arouse him from his dreamy indifference.

Not even when another and another sting of the same unusual kind caused him to renew his scratching—for by this time he was beginning to succumb to the narcotic influence that would soon induce the sleep of death.

It did thus end: for after a time, and almost without a struggle, the red-haired monster lay stretched upon the platform which had long been his resting-place, his huge limbs supple and tremulous with the last throes of life.

And beside him, in the same condition, was soon after seen his wife, who, of weaker conformation, had more quickly yielded to the soporific effect of the upas poison, from which, when it has once pervaded the blood, there is no chance of recovery.

Saloo did not deem the infant mias worthy a single arrow, and after its parents had been disposed of, he sprang upon the scaffold, followed by Captain Redwood, who, the moment after, was kneeling by his child, and with ear closely pressed to her bosom, listened to learn if her heart was still beating.

It was!

CHAPTER XXXVI.

AN IMPROVISED PALANQUIN.

"HE lives! thank God, she lives!"

These were the words that fell upon the ears of Henry and Murtagh, when Saloo, swimming back to the shore, related to them what had transpired. And more too. She had recovered from her swoon, a long-protracted syncope, which had fortunately kept her in a state of unconciousness almost from the moment of her capture to that of her rescue.

With the exception of some scratches upon her delicate skin, and a slight pain caused by the compression to which she had been subjected in that hideous hug, no harm had befallen her—at least no injury that promised to be of a permanent nature.

Such was the report and prognosis of Saloo, who had swam back to the shore to procure the ship-carpenter's axe, and his aid in the construction of a raft.

This was to carry Helen from the islet—from a spot which had so nearly proved fatal to her.

A bamboo grove grew close at hand, and with Saloo's knowledge and the ship-carpenter's skill, a large life-preserver was soon set afloat on the water of the lagoon. It was at once paddled to the islet, and shortly after came back again bearing with it a precious freight—a beautiful young girl rescued by an affectionate father, and restored to an equally affectionate brother.

Long before the raft had grounded against the shore, Henry, plunging into the shallow water, had gone to meet it, and mounting upon the buoyant bamboos, had flung his arms around the form of his little sister.

How tender that embrace, how fond and affectionate, how different from the harsh hostile hug of the monster, whose long hairy arms had late so cruelly encircled her delicate form!

As the child was still weak—her strength prostrated more by her first alarm when seized, than by aught that had happened afterward—Captain Redwood would have deemed it prudent to make some stay upon the shore of the lagoon.

But the place seemed so dismal, while the air was evidently damp and unhealthy, to say naught of the unpleasant thoughts the scene suggested, he felt desirous to escape from it as soon as possible.

In this matter the Malay again came to his assistance, by saying they could soon provide a litter on which the child might be transported with as much ease to herself as if she were travelling in the softest sedan-chair that ever carried noble lady of Java or Japan.

"Construct it, then," was the reply of Captain Redwood, who was altogether occupied in caressing his restored child.

Saloo needed no further directions: he only requested the assistance of Murtagh, along with what remained to him of his tools; and these being as freely as joyfully furnished, a score of fresh bamboos soon lay prostrate on the ground, out of which the palanquin was to be built up.

Lopped into proper lengths, and pruned of their great leaf-blades, they were soon welded into the shape of a stretcher, with a pair of long handles projecting from each end.

The palanquin was not yet complete, and by rights should have had a roof over it to shelter its occupant from rain or sun; but as there was no appearance of rain, and certainly no danger of being scorched by the sun in a forest where its glowing orb was never seen nor its rays permitted to penetrate, a roof was not thought necessary, and Saloo's task was simplified by leaving it a mere stretcher.

He took pains, however, that it should be both soft and elastic. The latter quality he obtained by a careful choice of the bamboos that were to serve as shafts; the former requisite he secured by thickly bedding it with the lopped-off leaves, and adding an upper stratum of cotton, obtained from a species of bombyx growing close at hand, and soft as the down of the eider-duck.

Reclining upon this easy couch, borne upon its long shafts of elastic bamboo, Saloo at one end and Murtagh at the other, Helen was transported like a queen through the forest she had lately traversed as a captive in a manner so strange and perilous.

Before the sun had set, they once more looked upon its cheering light, its last declining rays falling upon her pale face as she was set down upon the shore of the lake, beside that same tree from which she had taken her involuntary departure.

CHAPTER XXXVII.

THE JOURNEY CONTINUED.

THE captain's daughter, with the natural vigor of youth, soon recovered from the slight injuries she had sustained in her singular journey through the maze of boughs. The previous perils of shipwreck, and the various hairbreadth escapes through which she had more recently passed, made her last danger all the lighter to bear; for by these her child's spirit had become steeled to endurance, and her courage was equal to that of a full-grown woman. Otherwise the fearful situation in which she had been placed, if leaving life, might have deprived her of reason.

As it happened, no serious misfortune had befallen, and with Helen's strength and spirits both fully restored, her companions were able on the third day to resume their overland journey.

And still more, they started with a fresh supply of provisions—enough to last them for many long days. Captain Redwood and Saloo in their hunting excursion had been very successful. The captain had not been called upon to fire a single shot from his rifle, so that his slender store of ammunition was still good for future eventualities. Saloo's silent sumpits had done all the work of the chase, which resulted in the death of a deer, another wild pig, and several large birds, suitable for the pot or spit.

The hunters had been returning from their last expedition heavily loaded with game, when the cries of Helen, Henry, and Murtagh had caused them to drop their booty and hasten to the rescue.

Now that all was over, and they were once more reminded of it, Saloo and Murtagh went in search of the abandoned game, soon found it, gathered it again, and transported it to their camping-place by the side of the lake.

Here, during the time they stayed to await the recovery of Helen's health, the pork and venison were cut up and cured in such a manner as to insure its keeping for a long time—long enough indeed to suffice them throughout the whole duration of their contemplated journey; that is, should no unexpected obstacle arise to obstruct or detain them.

The fowls that had fallen to Saloo's arrows were sufficient to serve them for a few days, and with the fine supply of lard obtained from the carcass of the pig, they could be cooked in the most sumptuous manner.

In the best of spirits they again set forth; and it seemed now as if fate had at last grown weary of torturing them, and daily, almost hourly, involving one or other of them in danger of death.

From the edge of the lake, where their journey had been so strangely interrupted, they found an easy path across the remaining portion of the great plain.

Several times they came upon the traces of red gorillas, and once they caught sight of a member of the horrid tribe speeding along the branches above their heads.

But they were not so much afraid of them, after all; for Saloo admitted that he did not deem the *mias pappan* so dangerous; and he had ascertained that it was this species of ourang-outang they had encountered.

He confessed himself puzzled at the behavior of the one that had caused them so much fear and trouble. It was another species, the *mias rombi*, of which he stood in dread; and he could only account for the *mias pappan* having acted as it had done, by supposing the animal to have taken some eccentric notion into its head—perhaps caused, as we have already hinted, by its conflict with the crocodile.

Dangerous these gigantic *quadrumana* are, nev

ertheless;—their superhuman strength enabling them to make terrible havoc wherever and whenever their fury becomes aroused. But without provocation this rarely occurs, and a man or woman who passes by them without making a noise, is not likely to be molested.

Besides the large species, to which belonged the ape that had attacked them, the travellers saw another kind while passing across the plain. This was the *mias kassio*, much smaller in size, and more gentle in its nature.

But they saw nothing of those, tallest of all, and the most dreaded by Saloo—the *mias rombis*—although the old bee-hunter still maintained his belief that they exist in the forests of Borneo as well as in the wilds of Sumatra.

The plain over which they were making their way, here and there intersected with lagoons and tracts of tree-covered swamp, was the very locality in which these great apes delight to dwell; their habit being to make their huge platforms, or sleeping-places, upon bushes that grow out of boggy marsh or water—thus rendering them difficult of access to man, the only enemy they have need to dread.

CHAPTER XXXVIII.

THE FRIENDLY FLAG.

THE travellers had taken their departure from the lake-shore at an early hour of the morning; and before sunset they had traversed the remaining portion of the plain, and ascended a considerable distance up the sloping side of the mountains beyond.

Another day's journey, during which they accomplished a very long and tiresome march, brought them to the summit of the ridge, the great dividing chain which strikes longitudinally across the whole island of Borneo, so far as the geographers yet know it.

They could see far to the northward, dimly outlined against the sky, the immense mountain of Kini-Balu—which rises to a height of nearly 12,000 feet; but they derived their principal gratification from the fact that, in the country stretching westward, appeared nothing likely to prevent them from reaching the destined goal of their journey, the old Malay capital town of Bruni—or rather the isle of Labuan, which lies along the coast a little to the north of it, where Captain Redwood knew that a flag floated, which, if not that of his own country, would be equally as certain to give him protection.

From the position of Kini-Balu, whose square summit they could distinguish from all others, he could see the point to steer for as well, or even better, than if he had brought his ship's compass with him, and they would no longer be travelling in any uncertainty as to their course. From where they were it could be distinguished to a point, without any variation; and after a good night's rest upon the mountain-ridge, they commenced descending its western slope.

For a time they lost sight of the sun's orb, that, rising behind their backs, was hidden by the mountain mass, and casting a purple shadow over the forest-clad country before them. Soon, however, the bright orb, soaring into the sky, sent its beams before them, and they continued their journey under the cheering light.

Had it not been for fear of their fellow-beings, they would have advanced on without much further apprehension; for one and all were now rejoicing in a plentitude of restored health, and their spirits were consequently fresh and cheerful.

But they still had some dread of danger from man—from those terrible enemies, the Dyaks, of whom Bornean travellers have told such ghastly tales.

It seemed, however, as if our adventurers were not destined to discover whether these tales were true or false, or in any way to realize them. The evil star that had hung over their heads while on the eastern side of the island, must have stayed there; and now on the west nothing of ill appeared likely to befall them.

For all this they did not trust to destiny, but took every precaution to shun an encounter with the savages, travelling only at such times as they were certain the "coast was clear;" and lying in concealment whenever they saw a sign of danger. Saloo, who could glide through the trees with the stealth and silence of a snake, always led the advance; and thus they progressed from hill to hill, and across the intervening valleys, still taking care that their faces should be turned westward.

At length, after many days of this cautious progress, they ascended a steep ridge, which, rising directly across their route, made it necessary for them to climb it.

It caused them several hours of toil; but they were well rewarded for the effort. On reaching its summit, and casting their glances beyond, they saw below, and at a little to the left, the strange old wooden-walled town of Bruni; while to the right, across a narrow arm of the sea, lay the island of Labuan, and on its conspicuous buildings waved the glorious old banner of Britannia.

Captain Redwood hailed it with almost as much joy as if it had been the flag of his native land.

He was not then in the mood to dwell on any distinction between them; but, flinging himself on his knees, with Henry on one side, and Helen upon the other—Murtagh and the Malay a few paces in the rear—he offered up a prayer of devout and earnest gratitude for their great deliverance to Him who is ever powerful to save, their FATHER and their GOD.

THE END.

www.ingramcontent.com/pod-product-compliance
Lightning Source LLC
Chambersburg PA
CBHW031742230426
43669CB00007B/450